Together We Thrive:

ENGAGE
Involve
EMPOWER

by Nury Castillo Crawford

Copyright 2024
1010 Publishing LLC.

ISBN: 979-8-9858653-5-6

www.1010Publishing.com

For information about permission to reproduce selections from this book, email 1010PublishingUS@gmail.com, subject line, "Permission".

Almost 1 in 5 Americans,

62.6 million, are Hispanic,

according to the latest 2020

census numbers, a

23% increase from 2010.

(NBC News, September 15, 2022)

TABLE OF CONTENTS

Introduction

In the ever-evolving landscape of education today, the ever-changing increase of our multilingual learners, where the collaborative relationship between schools, families, and communities has gained unprecedented significance, the role of parents as essential partners in the academic journey of their children has never been more pivotal. Welcome to a comprehensive exploration of a paramount aspect of education: *Together We Thrive: Engage, Involve, Empower!* This 10-chapter book stands as a beacon of knowledge and guidance for educational public school leaders, illuminating the multifaceted dimensions of parental involvement, its profound impact on the achievement of our multilingual students, the intricate interplay of factors influencing parental engagement, and the innovative strategies that educational institutions and communities can harness to foster and enhance the quality and depth of parental involvement.

At the heart of this book lies a resolute commitment to uncovering the compelling connection between parental involvement and student achievement. With a wealth of research pointing to the remarkable correlation between active parental engagement and enhanced academic outcomes, educational leaders find themselves at a critical crossroads. In an era where the emphasis on personalized learning and holistic student development reigns supreme, the symbiotic partnership between schools and families emerges as a driving force behind sustainable scholastic success. As we navigate through chapters that delve into this integral link, we will traverse an array of empirical studies, revealing how parental involvement not only positively impacts academic performance but also contributes to cognitive growth, social-emotional development, and overall well-being of their children.

Yet, the road to fostering meaningful parental involvement is not without its intricate twists and turns. The book delves into a myriad of factors that influence parental engagement, recognizing the diversity of backgrounds, perspectives, and challenges that families bring to the table. From socioeconomic disparities to cultural nuances, the complexities that shape parental involvement are as diverse as the students and families themselves. By weaving together the threads of research, anecdotes, and expert insights, this book demystifies the intricate web of influences that shape the extent to which parents engage with their children's education.

As educational public school leaders embark on the journey of optimizing parental involvement, a rich tapestry of innovative strategies and best practices unfolds before them. Within the pages of each chapter, intricate blueprints are laid out, outlining approaches that transcend conventional boundaries and harness the power of technology, community partnerships, and proactive communication. This book not only equips leaders with a diverse toolkit of actionable strategies, but also offers a nuanced understanding of the critical role schools and communities play in creating an environment conducive to parental involvement.

However, this exploration goes beyond mere technique; it delves into the very essence of equity and inclusion that must permeate every facet of education. Recognizing the disparities that can hinder meaningful parental involvement, particularly among families originating from diverse backgrounds, the book ventures into uncharted territories, examining how schools can bridge the gap between home and school. By delving into case studies, research-driven insights, and on-the-ground experiences, this book lays the groundwork for a paradigm shift, fostering equitable practices that empower parents from all walks of life to be active participants in their children's educational journey.

In a world where educational transformation is the cornerstone of progress, *Together We Thrive: Engage, Involve, Empower!* can be used as a guide for educational public school leaders committed to building a brighter future. As each chapter unfolds, the intricate tapestry of parental involvement takes shape, revealing the profound impact it holds, the factors that shape its course, and the transformative strategies that can lead to its vibrant blossoming. With a resolute focus on fostering equitable practices, this book transcends traditional boundaries and invites leaders to embark on a transformative voyage, a journey towards nurturing an educational landscape where parents stand not as passive observers, but as dynamic collaborators in the holistic development of the leaders of tomorrow.

Embarking on this literary journey through *Together We Thrive: Engage, Involve, Empower!*, I am reminded of the decades I've spent immersed in the dynamic world of public education. My path has led me through more than 20 years of challenges and triumphs, where the pursuit of student achievement was inextricably linked with the commitment to parental and community engagement. In these pages, I share my personal journey of fostering collaboration, igniting transformation, and crafting an educational landscape where every stakeholder's voice resonates in the chorus of success.

My own journey began with a simple but profound realization: Education is a shared endeavor that transcends the confines of the classroom. I recognized that meaningful change could not be achieved by educators alone; it required a collective effort involving parents, families, communities, and beyond. This understanding became the cornerstone of my approach to education, infusing every facet of my work with the spirit of collaboration.

Parental and community engagement became a priority in every project I undertook. Drawing inspiration from pioneers in the field of education, I embraced the wisdom of other established experts such as Dr. Joyce Epstein, who emphasized that the connection between schools and families is integral to student success. I knew that to unlock the full potential of our students, we had to bridge the gap between home and school, transforming parents into partners and communities into allies.

However, achieving this vision wasn't without its challenges. Creative solutions were essential to make learning relevant and timely for all. I understood that every student came with a unique background, learning style, and set of circumstances.

One of the lessons I learned early on was the power of effective communication. I recognized that merely having ideas and solutions wasn't enough; the key was in delivering them in a way that resonated deeply. I firmly believed in the Rule of Seven: delivering a message seven times through seven different channels. Whether it was through newsletters, community meetings, social media, or face-to-face interactions, persistent communication was a cornerstone of my strategy.

Listening became equally vital. I valued the insights of parents, students, and community members, recognizing that their perspectives held the key to informed decision-making, ensuring that their voice was respected and valued. This open dialogue fostered a sense of ownership and co-creation, where the educational journey was a shared experience rather than a unilateral endeavor.

Throughout my journey, I witnessed firsthand the transformative power of collaboration. By championing parental and community involvement, I saw students thrive in ways previously unimagined. Academic success, confidence blossomed, and a culture of achievement took root. I have learned that success in parental involvement looks different for various school districts and even schools individually. Just like teaching and learning is individualized, so are your goals that focus on parental involvement. We have to meet the parents and community where they are.

As we delve into the pages of this book, I invite you to join me on a voyage through the principles, strategies, and insights that have shaped my journey and countless others in the field of education. The chapters ahead will unravel the multifaceted aspects of parental involvement, explore the factors that influence engagement, and provide a roadmap for fostering equitable practices. Through the lens of research, real-world examples, and the voices of pioneering scholars, we will forge a path toward transformative partnerships that nurture student success.

In sharing my experiences, successes, and challenges, I hope to inspire you to embrace the call to action reverberating through these pages. Just as I've learned, education is a collaborative symphony, and your unique role as an educational public school leader holds the potential to create lasting change. By fostering collaboration, embracing creativity, prioritizing communication, and persistently delivering the message of partnership, you have the power to empower families, elevate communities, and transform the trajectory of student success.

With unwavering dedication and the spirit of collaboration, let us embark on this transformative journey together, as we weave a narrative of empowerment, inclusion, and achievement that transcends time and leaves an indelible mark on the landscape of education.

Chapter 1: The Crucial Nexus of Parental Involvement and Student Achievement

In the intricate

ecosystem of education,

where the collective

pursuit of knowledge

and growth takes center stage, the profound influence of

parental involvement on student achievement stands as

an enduring testament to the power of collaboration. As

we embark on this enlightening journey into the heart of

Together We Thrive: Engage, Involve, Empower!, we are

called to explore the foundational connection that

underscores the entire narrative—the irrefutable link

between parental engagement and student achievement.

Latinos are one of the fastest growing and most racially

diverse students in American schools. The term *Latino*

generally refers to people with cultural ties to Latin America. It is commonly used to describe individuals or communities with roots in countries where the Romance languages, such as Spanish, Portuguese, or French, are spoken. *Latino* is often used as a broad and inclusive term encompassing diverse ethnicities, races, and nationalities within Latin America. It's important to note that *Latino* is a gender-neutral term when used to refer to individuals collectively. The feminine form is *Latina* when specifically referring to a woman. So, Latino can refer to both males and females when used in a general sense, while Latina is specifically used for females. These terms are widely used in the United States and other English-speaking countries to describe individuals of Latin American descent.

Driven by immigration, they account for more than 24 percent of the kindergarten to high school population. As noted by the National Center for Educational Statistics in May 2023 via their report titled "Racial/Ethnic

Enrollment in Public Schools". Despite their numbers, the achievement gap between Latinos and their non-Latino peers remains wide because they have the highest dropout rate. Knowing that Latinos are the second largest population in our public school system, I will focus on the Latino population in hopes to share some insight on how to best connect in meaningful relationships to support our students in reaching their full potential.

The journey begins by uncovering the transformative impact that parental involvement exerts on the academic journey of students. Extensive research across diverse educational contexts has consistently demonstrated a strong correlation between active parental engagement and improved student outcomes, per the American Psychological Association's research supported by various studies titled, "Parent Engagement in Schools". From elevated test scores and graduation rates to enhanced critical thinking skills and social development, the evidence is resounding: When parents are actively engaged in their children's education, the ripple effects are felt across the entire spectrum of student achievement. Yet, we are repeatedly faced with the resounding reality that parental involvement is not as strong as we would desire. This is not a specific challenge aligned to one demographic, but is varied; specific challenges can be aligned to the Latino immigrant community, to be more specific, to the first and second generation. Although the strategies and insight shared could be relevant to all families and communities. When strategizing on how to provide support, we must get to know more about the barriers such as the constructs of language proficiency, socioeconomic status, immigration status, and race/ethnicity. These variables pose challenges to Latino children and parents in U.S. society and its schools.

Delving deeper, we'll transcend the conventional confines of academic achievement and venture into the realm of holistic student development. The chapters ahead will reveal how parental involvement extends its benevolent touch beyond test scores and academic accolades, nurturing the very essence of each student's growth. From fostering a sense of self-efficacy and motivation to instilling invaluable life skills and resilience, the active partnership between parents and schools emerges as a dynamic force that shapes well-rounded individuals poised to thrive in an ever-evolving world.

The Landscape of Parental Involvement

To comprehend the true magnitude of this connection, however, it is imperative to acknowledge the intricate landscape that parental involvement traverses. Within educational diversity, factors ranging from cultural norms and socioeconomic status to language barriers and geographic location interplay influence the extent and nature of parental engagement. As educational leaders, your commitment to understanding and navigating these complexities serves as the cornerstone of fostering inclusive and effective partnerships.

Educational leaders stand as the trailblazers of change, entrusted with the noble mission of shaping an inclusive and empowering educational landscape. There are a few strategies we should keep in mind as we illuminate solutions through which educational leaders can navigate complexities, like language barriers, socioeconomic challenges, and cultural norms, to foster inclusive and effective partnerships with Latino families and students.

Navigating Complexity with Empathy

One of the foundational pillars of fostering inclusive partnerships is empathy. Educational leaders can commit to understanding the unique challenges faced by Latino families by immersing themselves in their narratives. Through active listening and open dialogue, leaders can create spaces where parents and families feel heard, valued, and understood. Hosting culturally sensitive forums that encourage sharing experiences and challenges can bridge the gap and lay the foundation for effective collaboration. Additionally, leaders can organize workshops or training sessions that provide insights into the cultural nuances and diverse backgrounds found within the Latino community. By fostering an environment that acknowledges and respects their rich tapestry of traditions and values, educators can better connect with parents. Moreover, incorporating bilingual communication strategies, such as translating important documents and announcements, demonstrates a commitment to breaking down language barriers and ensures that information is accessible to all, promoting a more inclusive and engaged school community. These deliberate efforts contribute to building trust and strengthening the partnership between educators and

Latino parents, ultimately enhancing the overall educational experience for their children.

Culturally Responsive Communication

Language barriers can pose significant challenges to meaningful engagement. To address this, educational leaders can prioritize the establishment of bilingual communication channels. By offering translated materials, multilingual workshops, interpreters during school events, and opportunities for families to lead, it creates an environment where language is not a barrier but a bridge to understanding. This approach empowers Latino families to participate actively in their child's education, to become active leaders, thus fostering a sense of ownership and partnership.

Strategic Resource Allocation

Socioeconomic challenges can hinder engagement for Latino families. Educational leaders can allocate resources strategically to address these barriers. Creating a resource hub that offers information about available community services, scholarships, and financial aid opportunities can empower families to overcome economic obstacles. Moreover, leaders can collaborate with local businesses and organizations to provide essentials such as school supplies, ensuring that every student has the tools they need to succeed. Ensuring the community is connected can also open doors for additional support systems for housing, food insecurities, and health wellness.

Cultural Proficiency Training

Cultural norms play a pivotal role in shaping how families engage with education. To navigate these norms effectively, educational leaders can provide cultural proficiency training to staff. This training equips educators with the skills to recognize, respect, and celebrate the diversity of cultural backgrounds. When teachers understand the cultural contexts of their students, they can create an inclusive classroom environment that validates students' identities and experiences. In this area, it is important to note that representation matters. In the context of a book focused on increasing parental engagement for Latino parents, *cultural norms* refer to the shared values, behaviors, and expectations that shape the way individuals within the Latino community interact and perceive their roles in family and society. These norms encompass a wide range of elements, including communication styles, family structures, traditions, and beliefs. Understanding and respecting these cultural norms is essential for educational leaders and practitioners seeking to engage Latino parents effectively. By acknowledging and incorporating cultural norms into their approach, educators can create a more inclusive and supportive environment, fostering positive relationships with Latino families and enhancing the overall educational experience for their children.

Creating a Collaborative Network

The complexities faced by Latino families often extend beyond the school gates. Educational leaders can collaborate with community organizations that serve Latino populations, creating a network of support that addresses a wide spectrum of needs. By partnering with local health centers, community centers, and immigrant support organizations, leaders extend their impact beyond academics, nurturing holistic well-being and success. In addition, media venues such as radio stations, television stations, and printed media could prove to be a successful strategy to explore.

Guided by the compass of research-driven insights and real-world examples, we chart a course towards cultivating a culture of collaboration that transcends traditional boundaries. This chapter introduces a treasure trove of innovative strategies and best practices that hold the potential to transform the way schools and communities engage with parents. From leveraging technology to amplify communication channels, to nurturing community partnerships that bridge the gap between home and school, these strategies will empower you to forge connections that resonate with the diverse array of families under your care. Social media plays an important role, as it is a mode of communication that crosses all cultural norms. As I am writing this chapter, I can share that WhatsApp has been such a huge resource, as it is widely used in Latin America. I can also confirm that if we take the time, and share the message more than seven times in seven different ways, other apps and or websites that your school district or school uses can also be effective. Texting for all of your students is an effective way to communicate, period. Nowadays parents might not acknowledge the text's receipt, but more than likely they will receive it. One way to garnish acknowledgment of communication is to incentivize doing so. It doesn't necessarily mean spending additional funds from limited budgets, as getting creative is the key. Community sponsors can donate funds or provide extrinsic motivation. Parents and families can serve as a bridge to connect with outside community supporters, as many personally know small business owners who can also benefit from joining forces with our schools.

As we traverse the contours of this exploration, the chapter culminates in a poignant reflection on equity and inclusion. Diverse families often encounter unique challenges in engaging with their children's education, a reality that underscores the urgency of fostering equitable partnerships. Through case studies and insights, we delve into actionable steps that dismantle barriers, amplify voices, and create a level playing field, ultimately paving the way for parental-involvement practices that resonate with the ethos of equality.

In the tapestry of *Together We Thrive: Engage, Involve, Empower!*, Chapter 1 serves as the foundational cornerstone, laying bare the intricate threads that weave together the undeniable connection between parental involvement and student achievement. As we journey deeper into the heart of this narrative, the subsequent chapters will unfurl layers of insight, research, and practical guidance, each contributing to the collective endeavor of fostering dynamic partnerships that stand as pillars of educational excellence and transformative growth.

In the intricate tapestry of education, the crucial nexus of parental involvement and student achievement weaves threads of support, guidance, and inspiration, creating a masterpiece of lifelong success. Just as a gardener tends to the soil nurturing growth, parents can cultivate the fertile ground of their child's potential, allowing brilliance to bloom.
—Nury Castillo Crawford

Chapter 2: The Dynamics of Parental Involvement: Exploring Models and Theories

In the intricate dance of education where the steps of student achievement are choreographed by collaborative efforts, the role of parents as partners takes center stage. As we continue our voyage through *Together We Thrive: Engage, Involve, Empower!,* Chapter 2 unravels the complexities of parental involvement through a lens of diverse models and theories. This chapter serves as a compass, guiding educational public school leaders through a myriad of conceptual frameworks that illuminate the dynamic interplay between parents, schools, and students.

Drawing inspiration from Bronfenbrenner's Ecological Systems theory, this section unveils the intricate layers that shape parental involvement. Just as ecosystems influence the growth of organisms within them, various systems—including the microsystem (family), mesosystem (school), exosystem (community), and macrosystem (cultural norms)–synergistically influence the extent and nature of parental engagement. By understanding this interconnectedness, educators gain a holistic perspective that informs strategies for nurturing robust partnerships which transcend boundaries. What could happen if a child's microsystem breaks down? If a child experiences conflict or neglect within their family, or bullying or rejection by their peers, their microsystem might break down. This can lead to a range of negative outcomes, such as decreased academic achievement, social isolation, and mental and physical health issues. Additionally, if the microsystem is not providing the necessary support and resources for the child's development, it can hinder their ability to thrive and reach their full potential.

Delving into Joyce Epstein's widely recognized framework, we explore the six distinct types of parental involvement: parenting, communicating, volunteering, learning at home, decision-making, and collaborating with the community. Each type represents a unique facet of parent-school interaction, shedding light on the multifaceted roles parents can assume to contribute meaningfully to their children's education. As educational leaders, embracing this framework empowers you to design targeted initiatives that cater to diverse parental strengths and preferences.

As educational leaders tasked with nurturing partnerships that transcend boundaries, we can use the Epstein Framework: Six Types of Involvement as a reference, knowing that when we incorporate it in our schools with Latino children enrollment, we will encounter unique challenges. In the context of fostering meaningful collaboration with Latino families, including first- and second-generation immigrants, this chapter delves into how educational leaders can seamlessly integrate this framework with my suggestions to help make it culturally relevant and timely. We should always remember to keep children as our priority as we make progress to create enduring partnerships that honor cultural diversity, language variations, and immigrant experiences.

1.   Parenting: Understanding Cultural Perspectives

As educational leaders, we can start by recognizing the importance of cultural parenting norms within Latino families. By offering workshops and resources that align with cultural practices and values, leaders empower immigrant parents to bridge generational gaps, while nurturing the growth of their children. Acknowledging that first- and second-generation immigrants often navigate dual identities, leaders can foster dialogue that values these intersections, creating an environment where diverse perspectives are celebrated. It's imperative for educators to first understand that the term *Latino* applies to those from many countries in Latin America, and that Latinos come in every race and can be multicultural as well. There are many similarities, but there are also complex differences found in regional celebrations, faith, and foods.

2. Communicating: Bilingual and Multimodal Outreach

Communication is pivotal in engaging Latino families, especially immigrants. Educational leaders can implement bilingual communication strategies that resonate with families from different linguistic backgrounds. Integrating technology, social media, and community forums allows leaders to deliver messages through diverse channels, ensuring that communication transcends language barriers. By offering translated materials and conducting regular check-ins, leaders bridge gaps and foster trust. Another strategy to keep in mind is both audio messaging and video messaging. This is where social media and the district website can assist. Some parents, depending on their own educational journey, are not proficient in Spanish when it is in the written format. Having recorded audio messages and video messages can help minimize that communication gap. We also have a small number of families whose proficient language is an indigenous one from their home country, and Spanish is their second language. Fliers and other modes of written communication that include visuals can help ensure the messages are received. Lastly, home visits, as they might not be as popular due to concerns of time, resources, and even safety, have proven to be effective when given as a choice to families. The more we communicate our message and the more ways we communicate, the better are the chances that the message will reach the household with which we are aiming to connect.

3. Volunteering: Inclusive Opportunities

For first- and second-generation immigrants, volunteering might be seen through a different cultural lens. Educational leaders can adapt volunteering opportunities to be inclusive of cultural norms, such as family-oriented events or collaborative projects. By offering flexible schedules that accommodate work demands, leaders empower immigrant parents to engage actively without sacrificing their commitments. Creating a safe space where their contributions are recognized and valued strengthens the partnership. We can also look for opportunities for parents to volunteer outside the school. We can ask parents to hand out fliers in their apartment complex to families they know, or even host a "Cafe con Leche" evening at their home. An evening meeting with a small group of families in a location that is familiar with them and close to where they live is always amenable. I began to integrate this as a quarterly event during my early years in school administration and visited with another staff member. It was never attended by more than a dozen parents, and there was no detailed agenda. It was just what the invitation said, "coffee and milk". Parents had the chance to use their voice to share wins and areas where they needed support. From this visit, we learned ways parents could help outside the school hours, such as sharpening pencils for the entire school right before standardized testing, helping spruce up the outdoor garden on weekends, and bringing treats for teacher appreciation week, to name a few.

4. Learning at Home: Culturally Relevant Resources

The Epstein Framework can be used to focus on learning at home and can be tailored to the experiences of immigrant families. Educational leaders can curate resources that not only align with academic goals but also respect cultural identities. By providing materials that promote multilingualism, cultural heritage, and the exploration of diverse perspectives, leaders empower Latino families to integrate learning seamlessly into their daily lives. This can include increasing titles that are culturally representative in the school library, to having a planning committee focus on Hispanic Heritage Month and having the automated phone message in a bilingual format. The best way I have found out how to ensure that families feel seen, heard, and respected is by asking them. Yes, through a survey that is printed at each event, or online via a QR code or social media; via "Cafe con leche" night, in addition to making sure all teachers include this inquiry when they have parent-teacher conferences or events. Different communities have different needs, so there is no correct answer here. If most of your Latino families are from the Caribbean Islands, their perspective will be different than those of the families from Mexico. You must get to know them, and take every opportunity to do so. It cannot be a "one time and you're done" type of situation, it must be consistent and evident that it is your goal to connect with them.

5. Decision-Making: Inclusive Participation

Leaders can integrate the Epstein Framework's decision-making aspect by ensuring that Latino families, including immigrants, have a seat at the table. By creating advisory councils that represent diverse backgrounds, leaders elevate the voices of immigrant parents in shaping policies and programs. Emphasizing the value of their insights and experiences fosters a sense of ownership and inclusivity.

The decision-making aspect of the Joyce L. Epstein's Framework involves including parents in the process of making decisions that affect the school and its programs. Educational leaders can integrate this aspect of the framework by ensuring the active participation of Latino families, particularly immigrants, in decision-making processes. The creation of advisory councils that reflect diverse backgrounds is proposed as a means to provide a platform for immigrant parents to contribute their perspectives.

In the strategic implementation of the Epstein Framework, leaders are encouraged to embrace the decision-making aspect as a cornerstone for fostering genuine collaboration with Latino families, especially those who are immigrants. Recognizing the pivotal role that diverse perspectives play in shaping educational policies and programs, leaders can proactively establish advisory councils that serve as dynamic platforms for representation. These councils must be meticulously designed to mirror the rich melting pot of backgrounds within the Latino community, ensuring a comprehensive and inclusive array of voices. Through this intentional inclusivity, leaders not only provide a seat at the table for immigrant parents, but also actively seek to amplify their voices in decision-making processes. By doing so, they not only acknowledge the unique challenges and valuable insights of Latino families, but also cultivate a sense of ownership and empowerment within these communities. Emphasizing the intrinsic worth of their experiences not only enriches the dialogue surrounding education, but also reinforces a collaborative ethos that is essential for the success of educational initiatives tailored to the needs of a diverse and vibrant community.

6. Collaborating with the Community: Cultural Capital

For immigrant families, the community holds immense significance. Educational leaders can tap into this cultural capital by forming partnerships with local immigrant support organizations, community centers, and cultural institutions. By collaborating on events, workshops, and celebrations, leaders create a bridge between school and community, fostering an environment where Latino families feel valued and connected.

Using the Epstein Framework for Involvement as a resource as we strive to support our schools' Latino families, particularly first- and second-generation immigrants, is a journey marked by empathy, cultural sensitivity, and adaptability. By embracing each of the six types of involvement and tailoring strategies to honor diverse experiences, educational leaders pave the way for transformative partnerships. These partnerships not only empower immigrant families to actively engage, but also contribute to the enrichment of the educational experience for all students, fostering a mosaic of unity, respect, and achievement.

The Socio-Cultural Perspective: A Lens of Cultural Capital

Within the realm of education, cultural capital plays a pivotal role in shaping parent involvement. This section delves into the socio-cultural perspective, which recognizes the influence of cultural background, language, and traditions on parent-school dynamics. By acknowledging and valuing the cultural capital that families bring to the educational table, educators can bridge the gap between home and school, fostering an environment that resonates with the rich medley of diverse communities. Everyone wants to feel seen, heard, and respected; enough cannot be emphasized for the need to feel like one belongs.

The Self-Determination Theory: Fostering Intrinsic Motivation

At the core of meaningful parental involvement lies intrinsic motivation—the internal drive to engage in the educational journey. When educators tap into the profound principles of the Self-Determination Theory, a transformative path emerges for schools to cultivate an environment that not only invites but nurtures parents' inherent motivation to participate actively in their children's education. Autonomy, the first pillar of the theory, emphasizes the significance of providing parents with a sense of control and choice in their involvement. This goes beyond traditional parent-teacher conferences; it involves empowering parents to contribute in ways that align with their skills, interests, and schedules. Competence, the second pillar, highlights the importance of fostering a sense of capability. Schools can offer workshops, resources, and ongoing support to enhance parents' knowledge and skills, enabling them to feel confident in their role as partners in education. Finally, relatedness, the third pillar, underscores the importance of building meaningful connections. Educators can facilitate opportunities for parents to connect with each other, forming a supportive community where experiences, challenges, and successes are shared. By addressing autonomy, competence, and relatedness, educators can inspire parents to take ownership of their roles, fueling a partnership rooted in genuine commitment and enthusiasm. This holistic approach not only strengthens the bond between schools and families but also lays the foundation for a collaborative educational journey where parents feel valued and integral to the success of their children.

The Digital Age: Technology as a Catalyst

In an era where technological advancements redefine communication and engagement, this section examines the transformative role of technology in parental involvement. From virtual parent-teacher conferences to online learning platforms, technology serves as a catalyst for amplifying connections between schools and families. By embracing digital tools thoughtfully, educators can overcome geographic barriers, enhance communication, and create opportunities for parents to be engaged participants in their child's educational journey.

As we navigate the intricate amalgam of parental involvement through the lens of diverse models and theories, Chapter 2 offers a panoramic view of the conceptual landscape. By embracing ecological systems, an adapted version guided by Epstein's Framework of Involvement, socio-cultural perspectives, the Self-

Determination theory, and the digital age, educational public school leaders are equipped with a nuanced understanding of the multifaceted dynamics that shape this pivotal partnership. Armed with this knowledge, the subsequent chapters beckon, inviting you to harness these insights as you craft strategies that empower parents as active agents of their children's academic success.

In the symphony of education, the dynamics of parental involvement compose harmonies that resonate through the corridors of learning, orchestrating a melody of collaboration, empowerment, and transformative growth. Like explorers of uncharted territories, we delve into models and theories, uncovering the treasure trove of insights that illuminate the path to educational excellence.

—Nury Castillo Crawford

Chapter 3: Unveiling the Research: The Impact of Parental Involvement on Student Achievement

In the symphony of education, where the harmonious interplay of various stakeholders shapes the melody of student success, the role of parents as active participants is a key crescendo. As we delve deeper into *Together We Thrive: Engage, Involve, Empower!*, Chapter 3 unveils a chorus of empirical research and insightful quotes that resoundingly attest to the profound impact of parental involvement on student achievement.

The Power of Partnership: A Research Odyssey

Venturing into the realm of educational research, we uncover seminal studies that leave an indelible mark, unequivocally affirming the transformative power of parental involvement. Dr. Joyce Epstein, a revered figure in education research and a fervent advocate of the six types of parental involvement, resounds this sentiment, emphasizing, "When families, schools, and communities collaborate, students not only attain elevated levels of achievement but also contribute to the overall effectiveness of their schools and communities" (Epstein, 2018). In her influential handbook, *School, Family, and Community Partnerships: Your Handbook for Action*, Dr. Epstein eloquently underscores the profound impact of united efforts in the educational journey.

Academic Attainment: A Co-Creative Journey

Delving into the wealth of research, the narrative unfolds with resonance, particularly in the works of Dr. William Jeynes, a distinguished Professor of Education at California State University. Dr. Jeynes articulates a compelling perspective on the intricate connection between parental engagement and academic achievement, highlighting that "parental involvement in education stands as a valuable asset, capable of serving as a transformative platform for students to ascend academically when effectively harnessed" (Jeynes, 2015). His insightful meta-analysis, titled "A Meta-Analysis: The Effects of Parental Involvement on Minority Children's Academic Achievement," not only underscores the significance of parental involvement, but also underscores its potential as a catalyst for the academic success of students from diverse backgrounds.

Beyond the Classroom: Social and Emotional Development

As the canvas of student achievement broadens beyond academic prowess, research demonstrates the role of parental involvement in nurturing social and emotional development. Dr. Nancy Hill, Professor of Education at Harvard University, highlights the holistic impact: "Engaged parents contribute to students' well-being by providing a safe and supportive environment that fosters the development of crucial socioemotional skills" ("Parent Involvement as a Lever for School Reform," 2009).

Bridging the Achievement Gap: An Equitable Promise

Embarking on an exploration of scholarly inquiries, I again encounter the illuminating work of Dr. William Jeynes. Drawing from my extensive experience in public education spanning over two decades, I wholeheartedly concur with Dr. Jeynes as he crafts a compelling narrative that resonates, shedding light on the profound relationship between parental engagement and academic attainment. Personally, I find resonance in his assertion that "parental involvement in education is not only a valuable asset but, when thoughtfully cultivated, can serve as a powerful platform for students, particularly within the Latino community, to soar academically" (Jeynes, 2015). In his enlightening meta-analysis mentioned previously, " Dr. Jeynes not only accentuates the universal importance of parental engagement, but also prompts a reflection on its specific implications for the academic success of students from the vibrant and diverse Latino community.

Amplifying Student Voice: A Unified Echo

In the symphony of educational research, the resonance of amplifying student voice through parental involvement emerges as a unifying theme. Reflecting on my extensive experience in public education for over two decades, I wholeheartedly endorse Dr. Sara Lawrence-Lightfoot's perspective on the transformative power of collaboration between parents and schools. Dr. Lawrence-Lightfoot, a distinguished sociologist and Professor at Harvard University, underscores that "when parents and schools collaborate, students witness a harmonious partnership that not only validates their experiences, aspirations, and voices but also cultivates a sense of belonging and empowerment within the learning environment" (Lawrence-Lightfoot, 2003). Personally, I find this stance particularly relevant to the Latino community, where fostering such collaborative partnerships can play a pivotal role in affirming the cultural richness, aspirations, and voices of students, thereby contributing to a more inclusive and empowering educational experience.

The Call to Action: A Resounding Consensus

From these insights, a resounding consensus emerges–the imperative for schools and communities to heed the call for increased and meaningful parental involvement. Researcher Anne Henderson and Karen Mapp underscore this directive: "Engaged parents, working in partnership with schools, hold the key to unlocking the doors of student achievement and success" ("A New Wave of Evidence: The Impact of School, Family, and Community Connections on Student Achievement," 2002).

In this collection of research, Chapter 3 underscores the undeniable impact of parental involvement on student achievement. The melodies of wisdom offered by eminent scholars serve as a guiding light, illuminating the transformative potential that lies within the collaborative partnership between parents, schools, and communities. As we continue our exploration, the subsequent chapters delve into the intricate factors that shape parental engagement and the innovative strategies that educational public school leaders can employ to foster and enhance this pivotal partnership.

In the gallery of academic progress, the unveiling of research unveils a masterpiece: the profound brushstrokes of parental involvement imbuing the canvas of student achievement with hues of empowerment, resilience, and boundless potential. With every study, we illuminate the corridors of understanding, crediting parents as co-authors in the story of their children's success.

—Nury Castillo Crawford

Chapter 4: Factors Shaping Parental Engagement: Unveiling the Complex Landscape

In the intricate tapestry of education, the threads of parental engagement are woven by a multitude of factors that intersect, each contributing to the unique fabric of collaboration between families and schools. As we delve further into the pages of *Together We Thrive: Engage, Involve, Empower!,* Chapter 4 unearths the diverse array of factors that shape parental engagement, drawing on research and insights from educational scholars and practitioners.

The Role of Socioeconomic Status

I conducted timely and relevant insight, as a leader in public education advocating for parental involvement, illuminating the pivotal influence of socioeconomic status on the extent and nature of parental engagement. What I learned emphasizes that "parents from lower socioeconomic backgrounds often face unique challenges, making it imperative for schools to offer tailored support that bridges the gap and empowers them as active partners in their children's education" (*Engaging Families in Schools: Community and Systemic Perspectives*, 2016).

Socioeconomic status (SES) can significantly impact parental involvement in Latino families, as it does in many other cultural groups. It's important to note that Latino families are not a homogenous group, and factors such as nationality, immigration status, and generational differences can also influence parental involvement.

However, there are some common ways in which SES can affect parental involvement in Latino families:

Time Constraints: Lower SES families often have limited time due to demanding work schedules and employment at multiple jobs to make ends meet. Both can lead to less time available for parental involvement in school activities, meetings, and helping with homework.

Language Barriers: In some cases, lower SES Latino parents may have limited proficiency in English, which can make it challenging to communicate with teachers and participate in school events. Language barriers can also affect their ability to help their children with schoolwork. This can also include limited written language proficiency in their home language. Language barriers can significantly hinder parental involvement in our school systems, creating a host of challenges for both parents and educators. When parents do not speak the primary language of the school or community, communication becomes strained, making it difficult for them to engage effectively in their children's education. This lack of communication can result in misunderstandings, missed opportunities for parental support, and limited access to vital information like school policies, academic progress, and extracurricular activities. Parents who are unable to understand or communicate with teachers may feel marginalized and disconnected from their children's educational experience.

Furthermore, they may hesitate to participate in parent-teacher conferences, school meetings, or volunteer activities due to the fear of embarrassment or frustration. Ultimately, language barriers can perpetuate a cycle of disengagement and hinder the collaborative efforts needed to ensure that every child receives the best possible education. To address this issue, schools should strive to implement strategies that promote effective communication, such as offering translation services, bilingual staff, and culturally sensitive outreach programs, to bridge these linguistic gaps and encourage parental involvement in the educational process.

Access to Resources: Families with higher SES tend to have greater access to educational resources like books, tutoring, and extracurricular activities, which can enhance parental involvement. Lower SES families might struggle to provide these resources. Limited access to resources can have a profound impact on parental involvement in our school systems, posing substantial challenges for both parents and educators. When parents lack access to essential resources such as transportation, childcare, or technology, their ability to actively engage in their children's education becomes compromised. For instance, parents without reliable transportation might struggle to attend school events, parent-teacher conferences, or meetings, inhibiting their participation in critical discussions about their child's progress. Similarly, parents who cannot secure affordable childcare during school events might find it challenging to attend, further restricting their involvement. Moreover, in an increasingly digital world, parents without access to necessary technology or internet connectivity might miss out on vital updates, homework assignments, and online resources shared by schools. This resource disparity can exacerbate educational inequities, making it difficult for parents to support their children effectively. To mitigate these challenges, schools should consider offering accessible alternatives, such as virtual meetings, flexible scheduling, transportation assistance, or on-site childcare services, to ensure that all parents, regardless of their resource limitations, can actively participate in their children's education and collaborate with educators for better academic outcomes.

Education Levels: Parents with higher education levels might feel more comfortable engaging with their children's school and advocating for their needs. Lower SES parents with lower levels of education might be less confident in their ability to navigate the education system. Limited educational levels among parents can significantly impact their involvement in our school systems, presenting unique challenges for both parents and educators. When parents have lower educational attainment, they might face difficulties in understanding and assisting with their children's schoolwork. This can lead to a lack of confidence in their ability to support their child's learning and engagement in school-related activities. Moreover, parents with limited education might feel intimidated by the educational system and be less likely to participate in parent-teacher conferences, school meetings, or volunteer activities due to a fear of not fully grasping the discussions or feeling out of place. In addition, parents with lower educational levels might struggle to navigate complex administrative processes, such as filling out forms, understanding school policies, or accessing educational resources, which can further hinder their involvement in their child's education and limit their ability to advocate for their child's needs within the school system. To address this issue, schools should adopt strategies that empower parents with lower educational levels. Providing clear and accessible communication materials, offering parental education programs, and creating a welcoming and non-judgmental environment can help parents feel more confident and capable of participating in their children's education. Moreover, educators can offer additional support and resources to help these parents understand and navigate the educational system, ensuring that they are equipped to play an active role in their child's academic journey.

Stress and Mental Health: Lower SES families often face higher levels of stress due to financial challenges and other life stressors. This can impact their mental health and overall well-being, making it more difficult to engage actively in their children's education. Stress and mental health challenges can significantly impede parental involvement in our school systems, creating a range of complex issues for both parents and educators. When parents are grappling with high levels of stress or facing mental health issues, their ability to actively engage in their children's education can be severely compromised. These individuals might struggle to find the emotional and mental capacity needed to support their child's learning effectively. The burden of stress or mental health challenges can lead to decreased motivation and energy, making it difficult for parents to attend school events, participate in parent-teacher conferences, or actively engage in discussions about their child's educational progress.

Furthermore, parents dealing with mental health issues might experience stigma and discrimination, which can discourage them from seeking help or engaging with the school community. Their concerns might also go unnoticed or unaddressed, potentially impacting their child's academic and emotional well-being. To address these challenges, schools must prioritize the mental health and well-being of *both* parents and students.

Offering accessible mental health resources and support services can help parents cope with stress and mental health challenges more effectively. Creating a welcoming and non-judgmental environment that encourages open communication about mental health issues can also reduce the stigma and encourage parents to seek help when needed. Additionally, schools can consider flexible engagement options for parents who might find traditional involvement methods overwhelming, such as virtual meetings or asynchronous communication channels.

Access to Information: Higher SES parents are more likely to have access to information about their children's school and educational opportunities. Lower SES parents might not be aware of available resources or how to access them. Limited access to information is a significant barrier that affects parental involvement in our school systems, and presents numerous challenges for both parents and educators. When parents do not have access to essential information about their child's education, they are unable to make informed decisions and actively engage in their child's learning journey. This can result in a lack of understanding about school policies, curriculum changes, and important academic dates, making it difficult for parents to provide the necessary support at home. Moreover, limited access to information can create disparities among families, with some parents being better informed than others due to factors such as socioeconomic status or language proficiency. This inequity can exacerbate educational inequalities and impact student outcomes. To address this issue, schools should prioritize transparent and inclusive communication practices. This includes providing information through multiple channels, such as emails, text messages, websites, and social media platforms, to accommodate diverse needs and preferences. Additionally, schools can offer translated materials for non-English-speaking parents, and ensure that information is accessible to parents with disabilities. Implementing user-friendly technology platforms can facilitate easy access to information, including grades, assignments, and school announcements. Educators and school staff should be proactive in reaching out to parents who might have limited access to information, and offer personalized support when necessary. Parental liaison programs or family engagement coordinators can bridge the gap by facilitating communication between the school and parents who face information access challenges.

Mobility: Economic instability can lead to frequent moves or housing instability, which can disrupt a child's education and make it harder for parents to stay involved. Limited access to mobility is a significant challenge that can hinder parental involvement in our school systems, posing distinctive obstacles for parents and educators alike. When parents face mobility constraints, such as a lack of reliable transportation, physical disabilities, or geographical distance from the school, their ability to actively participate in school-related activities can be severely restricted. This can include attending parent-teacher conferences, school meetings, or extracurricular events, all of which are crucial for fostering a strong partnership between parents and educators. Moreover, parents with limited mobility might struggle to be present in their child's school life in other ways, such as volunteering for school activities or attending school functions. This can leave them feeling isolated from the school community and disconnected from their child's educational experience. To address these challenges, schools should consider implementing inclusive and accessible approaches to parental involvement. This might involve offering virtual options for meetings and conferences, providing transportation assistance for parents who lack access to reliable transportation, or organizing school events in locations that are more accessible to all families. Schools can also create online forums and platforms for parents to engage in discussions and access resources remotely. In addition, educators and school staff should be sensitive to the unique needs of parents with limited mobility, and offer alternative ways for them to participate actively in their child's education. This might include sending materials home or finding creative solutions to involve parents in school activities, even if they cannot be physically present.

Cultural Factors: Cultural norms and expectations within the Latino community can influence parental involvement. Some Latino families might place a strong emphasis on the importance of education, and be highly involved in their children's schooling regardless of SES.

It's important to recognize that while SES can present barriers to parental involvement, many Latino families, regardless of their economic status, are highly committed to their children's education. Schools and communities can support parental involvement among lower SES Latino families by providing translated materials, offering flexible meeting times, and creating welcoming and inclusive environments that respect and value diverse cultural backgrounds. Efforts to bridge the gap between schools and parents from diverse socioeconomic backgrounds can help improve educational outcomes for Latino students.

Language and Cultural Diversity

Navigating the complexities of an ever-globalizing world, the dynamics of language and cultural diversity emerge as dual forces that not only enrich but also pose unique challenges to effective parental engagement. Drawing from my extensive two-decade tenure in public education, I unequivocally emphasize the paramount importance of embracing and celebrating linguistic and cultural diversity within educational settings. Based on my experiences, it is evident that schools committed to honoring diverse languages and cultural backgrounds create an inclusive environment, fostering a sense of belonging that empowers parents to engage authentically in their children's education. This aligns seamlessly with my own perspective presented in my insightful insightful interview for *Canvas Rebel* Magazine (Feb. 2023), highlighting the transformative impact of such inclusive practices on the engagement and empowerment of parents, particularly within the diverse compilation of the Latino community.

Communication and Information Accessibility

In the dynamic landscape of education, technology emerges as a potent force that simultaneously enriches and challenges parental engagement. With an extensive background spanning more than 2 decades in public education, my perspective strongly aligns with the transformative role of technology in fostering meaningful connections between schools and parents. Through firsthand experiences, I've observed how schools proficient in leveraging technology create innovative platforms for communication, collaboration, and involvement. My staunch belief is that embracing digital tools not only facilitates transparent and real-time exchanges, but also provides parents, particularly within the vibrant Latino community, with accessible avenues to actively participate in their children's educational journey. This viewpoint resonates deeply with insights shared by experts like the International Commission on the Futures of Education, as evidenced in their recent work "Reimagining Our Futures Together: A New Social Contract for Education" (2021), underscoring the pivotal role of technology in shaping a more inclusive and dynamic landscape for parental engagement.

These are some of the best strategies that I implemented and mentored other education leaders to implement as well. As leaders in public education, we can create a more inclusive and welcoming environment for diverse families, ultimately leading to improved student outcomes and a stronger sense of community within the school.

1. Cultural Competence Training: Education leaders and staff should receive training on cultural competence and sensitivity. This includes understanding the diverse backgrounds, values, and traditions of the families they serve.

2. Multilingual Support: Schools should provide information and communication in multiple languages spoken by the student population and their families. This includes translated documents, multilingual staff, and interpreters present for meetings.

3. Two-Way Communication: Establish open and ongoing channels of communication that encourage families to share their concerns, questions, and feedback. Ensure that families feel heard and respected.

4. Cultural Liaisons: Employ or designate cultural liaisons who can bridge cultural and linguistic gaps between the school and families. These liaisons can help families navigate the education system and connect with appropriate resources.

5. Regular Workshops and Information Sessions: Organize workshops and information sessions on topics relevant to parents, such as understanding the curriculum, college readiness, and parenting skills. Ensure that these sessions are accessible and accommodate different schedules.

6. Use of Technology: Leverage technology to communicate with families, such as through email, text messages, and educational apps. Make sure these tools are user-friendly and accessible to all.

7. Personalized Communication: Recognize that each family's needs and preferences may differ. Tailor communication methods to individual preferences whenever possible.

8. Parent-Teacher Conferences: Offer flexible scheduling for parent-teacher conferences to accommodate working parents. Provide interpreters if needed, and give parents a clear understanding of their child's progress and areas for improvement.

9. Family Engagement Programs: Develop family engagement programs that involve parents in school activities, decision-making processes, and volunteering opportunities. Encourage parents to participate in the school community.

10. Feedback Mechanisms: Create mechanisms for parents to provide feedback on school policies, programs, and practices. Act on constructive feedback to improve the educational experience.

11. Clear Communication of Expectations: Clearly communicate school expectations, including homework policies, attendance requirements, and behavioral expectations. Ensure that parents understand their role in supporting their child's education.

12. Celebrate Diversity: Celebrate and showcase the diversity within the school community through cultural events, displays, and activities that promote inclusivity and understanding.

13. Community Partnerships: Collaborate with community organizations and agencies that can provide resources and support to families, such as access to healthcare, housing assistance, and after-school programs.

14. Accessible Information: Make important school information, such as calendars, newsletters, and policies, readily available and easily understandable. Avoid jargon and use plain language.

15. Regular Updates: Provide regular updates on students' progress and any changes in school policies or procedures. Consistent communication helps parents stay informed and engaged.

Improving relevant communication with diverse families is essential for education leaders to foster stronger partnerships and ensure that all students receive the support they need. I'll expand on some of these strategies.

School Climate and Welcoming Spaces

The influence of the school environment on parental engagement cannot be overstated, especially when considering the distinct needs and dynamics of the Latino community. Rooted in my extensive experience of over 2 decades in public education, my perspective underscores the critical role schools play in tailoring their environments to resonate with the unique cultural contexts of Latino families. The nexus between a positive inclusive school climate and meaningful parental engagement becomes even more pronounced within this framework.

Delving into the realm of educational research, particularly insights from authoritative sources like *School, Family, and Community Partnerships: Your Handbook for Action* (2019), the consensus is clear: A welcoming atmosphere is paramount for fostering parental involvement. My experience aligns with this perspective, emphasizing that schools need to go beyond conventional approaches and proactively embrace strategies that resonate with the cultural diversity inherent in the Latino community. Creating an environment where families, particularly those from Latino backgrounds, feel not only welcomed but also respected as valued partners is crucial. By doing so, schools lay a solid foundation for cultivating authentic parent-school collaboration that goes beyond mere involvement to meaningful engagement.

Furthermore, the research underlines the need for schools to act as bridges between the diverse cultures represented in their student body and the educational experience. As someone deeply invested in promoting equity and inclusivity within education, I believe that schools must actively incorporate culturally responsive practices into their climate-building initiatives. Recognizing and celebrating the rich cultural heritage of Latino families fosters a sense of belonging and shared purpose. This intentional approach contributes to an atmosphere where parents feel empowered to engage meaningfully in their children's education, knowing that their unique perspectives and contributions are not only acknowledged but also integral to the collaborative educational journey.

Empowerment and Inclusivity

At the core of empowering parents within the educational landscape, particularly within the nuanced context of the Latino community, lies the imperative of cultivating an inclusive and collaborative culture. Rooted in my extensive background of more than 2 decades in public education, I draw inspiration from personal experiences that underscore the transformative impact of educational institutions embracing parents as equal stakeholders. Within this framework, the recognition and valuing of diverse perspectives and contributions catalyze a shift from mere passive participation to robust active engagement.

The resonance of this perspective becomes particularly pronounced when considering the unique needs and aspirations of Latino families. In my journey, I have witnessed firsthand how fostering an inclusive and collaborative culture within educational institutions creates a conducive environment for parents, especially those from Latino backgrounds, to feel not only welcomed but truly empowered. This goes beyond a mere acknowledgment of parents as partners; it involves actively incorporating their voices into the decision-making processes, understanding and respecting their cultural norms, and recognizing the wealth of experiences they bring to the educational table.

The insights gleaned from authoritative sources, such as *Parent Engagement for Student Success: A Guide for K-12 Educators* (2014), echo this sentiment, emphasizing the pivotal role of an inclusive and collaborative culture in the empowerment of parents. In aligning my own experiences with this perspective, I emphasize that educational institutions must go beyond superficial measures and embrace systemic changes that reflect a genuine commitment to inclusivity. This includes fostering a two-way communication channel that respects and values the unique contributions of parents from diverse backgrounds, particularly within the vibrant and diverse Latino community.

As an advocate for equity and inclusivity, I firmly believe that the cultivation of an inclusive and collaborative culture is not only essential for empowering parents, but also serves as a catalyst for creating educational environments where the diverse voices and perspectives of Latino families are not only acknowledged but actively contribute to shaping the educational journey. By recognizing parents as equal partners and proactively involving them in the collaborative processes of education, institutions can foster a sense of ownership and shared responsibility, ultimately leading to more meaningful and successful educational outcomes for all students.

Empowering diverse families in parental involvement requires a proactive and culturally sensitive approach. Schools should continually assess their efforts, solicit feedback, and adapt their strategies to meet the evolving needs of their diverse student body and families. When families are empowered and engaged, it positively impacts student achievement and the overall school community. It is imperative that we are cognizant of the impact it can make in fostering a successful learning environment for all students.

1. **Cultural Competence:** School staff, including teachers and administrators, should receive training on cultural competence and awareness. Understanding and respecting the diverse

backgrounds, values, and traditions of families is essential for building trust.

2. A Welcome and Inclusive Environment: Create a welcoming and inclusive school environment where all families feel valued and respected. Display diverse cultural symbols and promote tolerance and acceptance.

3. Cultural Liaisons and Support: Employ or designate cultural liaisons or family support specialists who can bridge cultural and linguistic gaps between the school and diverse families. These individuals can provide guidance and assistance to families.

4. Effective Communication: Establish clear and open lines of communication with families. Communicate through various channels, including newsletters, email, text messages, phone calls, and social media, in multiple languages as needed.

5. **Parental Leadership Programs:** Develop and support parental leadership programs that empower parents to take on leadership roles within the school community. Encourage them to serve on advisory boards, parent-teacher associations, and other decision-making committees.

6. **Education and Workshops:** Offer workshops and training sessions tailored to the specific needs and interests of diverse families. Topics may include understanding the education system, advocating for their child's needs, and improving parenting skills.

7. **Family Resource Centers:** Establish family resource centers within the schools or nearby locations where families can access information, resources, and support services, such as tutoring, counseling, and healthcare referrals.

8. **Flexible Meeting Times:** Recognize that diverse families may have different work schedules and family commitments. Offer flexible meeting times for parent-teacher conferences, workshops, and school events to accommodate their availability.

9. **Parental Mentor Programs:** Implement mentorship programs where experienced parents can guide and support newcomers in the school community. This can help build a sense of belonging and confidence among diverse families.

10. **Community Partnerships:** Collaborate with community organizations and agencies that provide services and resources relevant to the needs of diverse families. These partnerships extend the support network beyond the school.

11. **Feedback Mechanisms:** Create mechanisms for families to provide input and feedback on school policies, programs, and practices. Act upon

constructive feedback to demonstrate that their opinions are valued.

12. Celebrating Diversity: Organize cultural events, festivals, and diversity celebrations within the school. Encourage families to share their cultural traditions, foods, and stories with the school community.

13. Parental Engagement Plans: Develop and implement formal parental engagement plans that outline goals, strategies, and activities for involving diverse families in the school community.

14. Access to Resources: Ensure that all families have equitable access to educational resources, including books, technology, and tutoring services, to support their child's learning.

15. Recognize and Showcase Success Stories: Highlight success stories of diverse families and students within the school community to inspire and motivate others.

Navigating Complexities: A Unified Effort

In the symphony of factors that shape parental engagement, the voices of scholars and practitioners echo a unified call for collaborative efforts. Dr. Anne T. Henderson, a prominent advocate for family engagement, emphasizes that, "it takes a village to nurture successful parental involvement—schools, families, and communities must work together harmoniously, recognizing, and addressing the multifaceted factors that influence engagement" ("A New Wave of Evidence: The Impact of School, Family, and Community Connections on Student Achievement," 2002).

Chapter 4 offers a panoramic view of the intricate landscape that informs parent engagement. The insights of researchers and practitioners illuminate the multifaceted factors that shape this pivotal partnership from socioeconomic influences and linguistic diversity to communication strategies and the cultivation of empowering school environments. As we journey forward, the subsequent chapters unfold strategies and approaches that educational public school leaders can adopt to promote equitable and meaningful parental involvement, bridging the gap between home and school.

In the intricate tapestry of education, the threads of parental engagement are woven by a myriad of factors, forming a complex landscape where passion, culture, communication, and collaboration converge. As we navigate this mosaic of influences, we illuminate the path to meaningful partnership, acknowledging that understanding these factors is the compass that guides us toward nurturing thriving educational ecosystems.

—Nury Castillo Crawford

Chapter 5: Strategies for Meaningful Parental Involvement: Fostering Lasting Partnerships

As the canvas of education continues to evolve, the imperative for meaningful parental involvement stands as a cornerstone of transformative progress. In the heart of *Together We Thrive: Engage, Involve, Empower!*, Chapter 5 unfurls a mosaic of innovative strategies and real-world examples, equipping educational public school leaders with actionable approaches to foster lasting partnerships that transcend conventional boundaries.

Cultivating Two-Way Communication

At the core of effective parental involvement lies a commitment to open and two-way communication. Dr. Karen Mapp's wisdom underscores this significance: "Creating platforms for dialogue, where parents' voices are heard and valued, establishes a culture of partnership where shared insights lead to holistic student success" (*Beyond the Bake Sale: The Essential Guide to Family-School Partnerships,* 2007).

Incorporating two-way communication between schools and parents of diverse communities, including Latino families, is essential for building strong partnerships and improving student outcomes. Here are some proven best practices for achieving effective two-way communication:

Cultural Competence and Sensitivity:
- Provide training to school staff to enhance their cultural competence and sensitivity,

helping them understand the diverse backgrounds and values of Latino families.

- Promote respect for cultural differences and create an inclusive environment where all families feel valued.

Multilingual Communication:

- Offer communication in multiple languages spoken by the community, including translated documents, websites, and signage.
- Employ multilingual staff or interpreters to assist with communication during meetings, conferences, and events.

Parent-Teacher Conferences:

- Schedule parent-teacher conferences at convenient times for working parents, including evenings and weekends.

- Provide interpreters or bilingual staff to facilitate conversations between parents and teachers.
- Offer clear information about a student's progress, strengths, and areas for improvement, and discuss strategies for improvement.

Regular Updates and Newsletters:

- Send regular updates and newsletters to parents that highlight important school events, achievements, and opportunities.
- Include information on how parents can support their children's learning at home.

Open Houses and Workshops:

- Host open houses and workshops that allow parents to familiarize themselves with the school environment, curriculum, and educational goals.

- Provide workshops on topics of interest, such as college readiness, homework assistance, and parenting skills.

Parental Advisory Committees:

- Establish parental advisory committees that include representatives from diverse communities, including Latino families.
- Use these committees to gather input on school policies, programs, and initiatives.

Parent-Teacher Associations (PTAs):

- Encourage diverse parental participation in PTAs and other parental organizations.
- Ensure that these groups reflect the cultural and linguistic diversity of the school community.

Digital Communication:

- Utilize digital tools, such as email, text messages, and social media, to keep parents informed about school events, deadlines, and important updates.

- Ensure that online platforms are accessible and user-friendly for all parents.

Parental Surveys and Feedback:

- Conduct surveys to gather feedback from parents on their communication preferences and areas where they need more support.
- Act on the feedback received, and communicate the changes made in response to parental input.

Parent-Teacher Communication Apps:

- Implement apps or platforms that facilitate direct communication between parents and teachers.
- Encourage teachers to use these tools to share updates on assignments, class activities, and student progress.

Student-Led Conferences:

- Consider student-led conferences where students take an active role in discussing their progress and goals with their parents and teachers.

Community Engagement:

- Collaborate with community organizations that serve Latino families to strengthen the school's connection with the broader community.

- Hold events and workshops in partnership with community organizations to address common challenges and concerns.

Personalized Support:

- Offer individualized support to parents who might face unique challenges, such as parents of students with special needs or recent immigrant families.

Celebrating Cultural Diversity:

- Organize events that celebrate the cultural diversity of the school community, including cultural festivals, heritage months, and multicultural showcases.

Conflict Resolution Resources:

- Provide resources for conflict resolution and mediation for parents who might encounter challenges or disputes with school staff or policies.

Family Workshops and Learning Opportunities

Empowering parents as partners necessitates the provision of opportunities for growth and learning. Dr. Anne T. Henderson's research accentuates the impact of family workshops: "Engaging parents in workshops that provide insights into curriculum, teaching methodologies, and ways to support learning at home amplifies their capacity to actively contribute to their child's academic journey" ("A New Wave of Evidence: The Impact of School, Family, and Community Connections on Student Achievement," 2002).

Parent-Led Initiatives and Committees

Fostering a sense of ownership within parents is crucial for sustained engagement. For more than 2 decades, I witnessed the results of empowering parents to lead committees or initiatives fosters a sense of agency, enabling them to co-create solutions and actively contribute to the school's vision. This strategy is reiterated by Dr. Joyce Epstein (*School, Family, and Community Partnerships: Your Handbook for Action*, 2019).

Parent-led committees and initiatives in public schools can achieve significant success for various reasons. They signify high levels of parental engagement, which correlates with improved student outcomes. These committees bring together diverse perspectives, reflecting a broad range of backgrounds and experiences among parents. This diversity often leads to innovative solutions that benefit all students. Additionally, parent-led initiatives foster a sense of community within the school, promoting relationships and shared responsibility for student success. These groups can advocate for students, voice concerns, and advocate for improvements in curriculum, resources, and policies. Moreover, they often mobilize valuable resources, including funding, volunteers, and expertise, while focusing on issues that directly align with parental priorities. This involvement promotes transparency, collaboration between parents and teachers, and a lasting commitment to educational improvement, ultimately benefiting the entire school community.

Leveraging Technology for Inclusivity

In the digital age, technology becomes a potent tool for fostering inclusivity. I will admit that I celebrated the opportunity, and I genuinely emphasize the transformative potential of technology: "Utilizing digital platforms for communication and virtual involvement ensures accessibility for all families, transcending geographical barriers and inviting diverse voices into the educational discourse" (*Engaging Families in Schools: Community and Systemic Perspectives*, 2016).

Leveraging technology for inclusivity in public schools is a crucial strategy to increase parental involvement. In today's digital age, technology can bridge communication gaps, making it easier for diverse families, including those with limited time or language barriers, to engage with their child's education. Schools can utilize email, text messaging, dedicated school apps, and websites to provide parents with real-time updates on their child's progress, upcoming school events, and important announcements. Virtual meetings and webinars enable parents to participate in school activities and parent-teacher conferences even if they cannot be physically present. Moreover, technology can offer translation services, ensuring that information is accessible to non-English-speaking parents. By making information readily available and accessible through technology, schools can create a more inclusive environment that empowers parents to actively support their children's education, regardless of their backgrounds or constraints.

Home-School Collaboration in Action: An Example

Lincoln Elementary School's* Innovative Parental Involvement Program is one I want to share with you. In the last decade, Lincoln Elementary School, located in a diverse urban community, implemented an innovative parental involvement program that showcased the power of collaboration between parents and educators. Recognizing the importance of engaging parents in their children's education, Lincoln Elementary launched a multifaceted approach.

They introduced a user-friendly mobile app, "Lincoln Connect," which allowed parents to access their child's academic progress, communicate directly with teachers, and receive real-time notifications about school events and updates. The app was available in multiple languages to cater to the diverse population of parents.

Additionally, Lincoln Elementary established a Parent-Teacher Association (PTA) that not only organized traditional events, but also introduced workshops on topics like college readiness, digital literacy, and parenting skills. These workshops addressed the specific needs and interests of parents, making them more accessible and relevant.

Furthermore, the school held regular "Parent-Teacher Conferences for All," providing opportunities for all parents, regardless of work schedules or language proficiency, to meet with teachers. Bilingual interpreters were available during these conferences to facilitate communication.

Over the course of the decade, Lincoln Elementary saw a significant increase in parental involvement. Parental attendance at school events and PTA meetings surged, and more parents were actively using the "Lincoln Connect" app to engage with their child's education. As a result, students at Lincoln Elementary experienced improved academic performance, and the school community became more tightly knit.

The experience with this school illustrates the impact of a comprehensive approach to parental involvement in a diverse public school setting, showcasing the potential benefits of such initiatives. Real-world success stories often share similar features, demonstrating the importance of engaging parents as partners in their children's education.

Nurturing Cultural Responsiveness

Cultural responsiveness serves as a guiding principle in fostering meaningful partnerships. I want to offer my insights and offer a guiding light: Cultivating cultural responsiveness within educational institutions creates a safe space where parents feel valued, their perspectives are embraced, and their diverse contributions are celebrated.

Nurturing cultural responsiveness in schools can significantly enhance parental involvement by creating a more inclusive and welcoming educational environment. When schools actively acknowledge and respect the diverse cultural backgrounds and values of their students and families, parents from all backgrounds are more likely to feel valued and respected. This sense of inclusion encourages greater participation in school activities, meetings, and initiatives. Schools that prioritize cultural responsiveness often provide materials and communications in multiple languages, ensuring that language barriers do not hinder parents' access to information and engagement opportunities. Furthermore, culturally responsive schools are more attuned to the unique needs and expectations of diverse families, fostering trust and mutual understanding. As a result, parents are more motivated to become active partners in their children's education, leading to improved academic outcomes and stronger school communities.

The Collaborative Journey Ahead

In the symphony of strategies, I echo a guiding mantra: "Empowering parents requires an unwavering commitment to inclusivity, a shared vision, and a collaborative spirit. When schools, families, and communities unite, the possibilities for student achievement are boundless." This quote underscores the fundamental principles of effective education. To empower parents means recognizing that they are essential partners in their children's educational journey. It begins with a commitment to inclusivity, ensuring that all families, regardless of their backgrounds or circumstances, have a voice and a place in the educational process. A shared vision, which aligns the goals of schools, families, and communities, forms the basis for collaborative efforts. When these stakeholders unite, they create a supportive ecosystem that provides students with the resources, encouragement, and guidance they need to thrive both academically and personally. In such an environment, the potential for student achievement truly knows no bounds, as it capitalizes on the collective wisdom, care, and dedication of everyone involved in a child's education.

Chapter 5 is an expedition into the realm of actionable strategies, supported by the insights of visionary researchers. Through the prism of quotes and case studies, this chapter equips educational public school leaders with a toolkit of approaches that amplify parental involvement, nurturing partnerships that transcend barriers and flourish within the mosaic of holistic student success. As we proceed, the subsequent chapters will delve into the challenges faced by families from diverse backgrounds, and explore recommendations for fostering equitable parental involvement practices, ensuring that every voice resonates within the chorus of collaboration.

In the symphony of education, the strategies for meaningful parental involvement compose harmonies that resonate beyond the classroom, fostering partnerships that echo with trust, communication, and shared aspirations. Just as a skilled conductor orchestrates a masterpiece, educators and parents collaborate to create a symphony of learning, where every note played nurtures the melody of a lifelong journey.
—Nury Castillo Crawford

Chapter 6: Transforming Schools through Intensive Parental Involvement: A Case of Triumph

In the realm of education, tales of triumph emerge as beacons of hope, illuminating the transformative power of dedicated parental involvement. Chapter 6 of *Together We Thrive: Engage, Involve, Empower!* delves into the inspiring journey of a turnaround school in the United States, situated within a low socio-economic area, that harnessed the force of parental engagement to achieve remarkable academic gains.

A Glimpse into Hope Academy: A Turnaround Story

One notable example of a turnaround school that implemented strategies to improve both parental involvement and student academic success is the Mary E. Sampson Elementary School. A decade ago, this school faced numerous challenges, including low student achievement, a lack of parental engagement, and a diverse but disconnected community. Recognizing the need for change, the school embarked on a transformative journey.

First, the school established a welcoming and inclusive environment by actively embracing its cultural diversity. They hired bilingual staff, provided translated materials, and celebrated cultural events to make all families feel valued. They also introduced regular "Family Learning Nights" that featured workshops and activities designed to strengthen the home-school connection.

To enhance communication, Sampson Elementary introduced a user-friendly mobile app that allowed parents to track their child's academic progress, receive homework assignments, and communicate directly with teachers in multiple languages. The app helped bridge language barriers, and gave parents real-time access to their child's education.

Furthermore, the school revitalized its Parent-Teacher Association (PTA) with a focus on community building. They organized events that encouraged family involvement and provided opportunities for parents to volunteer in various capacities, including tutoring and mentoring.

Over the years, the efforts bore fruit. Parental involvement at Sampson Elementary significantly increased, resulting in more parents attending school events, participating in PTA meetings, and engaging with teachers. The positive outcomes extended to student performance, with standardized test scores showing consistent improvement. Students began to excel academically, and the school's overall culture shifted from disconnected to closely knit, fostering a sense of shared responsibility for student success.

The Mary E. Sampson Elementary School's turnaround serves as a compelling example of how a concerted effort to improve parental involvement, coupled with a focus on inclusivity and community building, can lead to remarkable academic success and a thriving school environment. (*Sampson County Schools continues to meet growth*, The Sampson Independent, 2016)

Empowerment as the Cornerstone

At the helm of this transformational journey, the school principal and I worked together to create a 5-year strategic plan to ensure we knew the specific tasks that needed to be done, and we collected data and noted who would be accountable for each task. The work with the school principal helped me gain more knowledge and understanding, and allowed me to connect with other champions of parental involvement throughout the country. Recognizing that the socio-economic challenges families faced often translated into barriers to involvement, the school principal implemented innovative strategies to empower parents as active partners. Quarterly workshops were established, focusing on equipping parents with skills to support learning at home and engage meaningfully in their child's education.

Collaboration Breeds Success

A pivotal turning point came with the implementation of the 5-year strategic plan created to increase parental involvement. The school principal, inspired and motivated by the initial small wins, believed that a collaborative approach would amplify parental involvement. The plan included the inclusion and collaboration by comprising parents, teachers, and community members. This served as a dynamic platform for dialogue, where ideas were exchanged, challenges addressed, and solutions co-created. This ensured that the community, including parents, had a voice resulting in feeling seen, heard, and respected. In this way, the changes needed were not given by the school or school leaders. It was a collected effort and relevant solutions were implemented by the representative members of the school community.

Tailored Support and Resources

Hope Academy's journey showcased a commitment to overcoming barriers. The school principal embraced insights and timely feedback, and recognized that communication and accessible information were vital. The school introduced a bilingual newsletter, regular text message updates, and virtual parent-teacher conferences to ensure parents were informed and engaged, regardless of language or work schedules.

Uniting for Academic Gains

The results of Hope Academy's transformation were nothing short of astonishing. Within 3 years, the school witnessed a 40-percent increase in standardized test scores. The school principal and her team attribute this success to the unwavering dedication of parents who rallied behind their children's education. The collaborative initiatives, workshops, and open communication lines created a sense of unity where parents, teachers, and students worked together to achieve academic excellence.

A Blueprint for Empowerment

The remarkable journey of Hope Academy serves as a blueprint for schools across the nation seeking to harness the potential of intensive parental involvement. The school principal's relentless dedication, inspired by the insights of pioneering educators, showcased that even in the face of socio-economic challenges, parental engagement can be a driving force for positive change. The story of Hope Academy reiterates my conviction: "When parents are empowered as partners, the potential for educational transformation is limitless."

In Chapter 6, the narrative of Hope Academy paints a vivid portrait of triumph over adversity. The story underscores the transformative impact of intensive parental involvement in a low socio-economic area, serving as an inspiring testament to the potential of collaboration between schools, families, and communities. As we continue our journey, the forthcoming chapters will delve into the challenges faced by families from diverse backgrounds and provide recommendations for cultivating equitable parental involvement practices that empower all stakeholders in the education landscape. (Area School Study Haps Model, Hope Academy of Public Service 2019).

In the grand narrative of educational transformation, the case of triumph through intensive parental involvement stands as a testament to the alchemical power of collaboration. With parents as co-authors, schools are transmuted into vibrant hubs of growth, where dedication, innovation, and unity reshape the very essence of learning. This remarkable journey of transformation credits the dedication and synergy between educators, parents, and students.

—Nury Castillo Crawford

Chapter 7: Bridging the Equity Gap: Empowering Diverse Families through Inclusive Parental Involvement

In the diverse amalgam of modern education, the pursuit of equity stands as a moral imperative, compelling educational leaders to dismantle barriers and nurture an environment of inclusivity. As we delve into the heart of *Together We Thrive: Engage, Involve, Empower!,* Chapter 7 takes a profound exploration into the challenges faced by families from diverse backgrounds, and illuminates strategies for fostering equitable parental involvement practices that bridge the gap between home and school.

The Intersection of Diversity and Equity

The path to equitable parental involvement requires a sensitive understanding of the intersection between diversity and equity. Dr. Gloria Ladson-Billings, a pioneering scholar in multicultural education, emphasizes that, "schools must recognize and celebrate the diverse backgrounds of families, acknowledging that cultural competence is the foundation upon which inclusive parent involvement is built" (*The Dreamkeepers: Successful Teachers of African American Children*, 1994).

Overcoming Language Barriers

Language serves as both a conduit and a barrier for effective parent-school collaboration. Dr. Patricia Gándara's research underscores that, "schools must prioritize bilingual communication, translation services, and culturally relevant resources to ensure that language differences do not hinder parents' ability to engage meaningfully in their child's education" (*The Bilingual Advantage: Language, Literacy, and the US Labor Market*, 2014).

Cultivating Cultural Responsiveness

Cultural responsiveness takes center stage in fostering an environment where all families feel welcomed and valued. Dr. Django Paris, an expert in culturally sustaining pedagogy, asserts that, "schools must not only tolerate but embrace the cultural identities of families, creating spaces where diverse perspectives enrich the educational dialogue and empower parents as active contributors" (*Culturally Sustaining Pedagogies: Teaching and Learning for Justice in a Changing World*, 2017).

Family-School-Community Partnerships

The cornerstone of equitable parental involvement lies in building robust family-school-community partnerships. Dr. Joyce Epstein's seminal work underscores the significance of these partnerships: "Collaborative efforts that extend beyond the school gates, incorporating community organizations and local resources, amplify the impact of parent involvement, nurturing an ecosystem of shared responsibility" (*School, Family, and Community Partnerships: Your Handbook for Action*, 2019).

Empowering through Resource Allocation

Equity in parental involvement extends beyond cultural responsiveness to resource allocation. Dr. Ann M. Ishimaru's research emphasizes that, "schools must allocate resources to support families from diverse backgrounds, ensuring access to workshops, materials, and opportunities that enable all parents to actively engage in their child's education" (*Equity Walks: Exploring Equity and Justice in School and Society*, 2019).

A Success Story: The Multilingual Family Center

Examining a real-world success story, the Multilingual Family Center (MFC) on the west coast, emerges as a beacon of equitable parental involvement. The MFC, inspired by my collaboration with the school district focused on the principles of empowerment, offered comprehensive support for families from diverse linguistic backgrounds. By providing bilingual workshops, cultural celebrations, and community engagement events, the MFC fosters a nurturing space where families collaborate with educators to enhance student success.

A multilingual family center integrated within a school plays a pivotal role in supporting diverse communities, by providing essential resources and information to empower families and enhance students' education. Such a center offers language accessibility, ensuring that parents of diverse linguistic backgrounds can access crucial information related to their child's education, school events, and district policies. It provides translation services for important documents, facilitates communication between teachers and parents, and offers language workshops to help parents improve their English proficiency. Additionally, the family center offers workshops and information sessions on a range of topics, including navigating the education system, understanding curriculum and grading, and accessing community resources like healthcare and social services. It may also host parent-teacher conferences, enabling meaningful dialogues between parents and educators. Ultimately, a multilingual family center fosters a welcoming and inclusive atmosphere, empowering families to actively engage in their children's education and creating a strong, supportive school community.

The Call to Equity: A Unified Vision

In the symphony of strategies for equitable parental involvement, the voices of scholars and practitioners harmonize in a call to action. Dr. James P. Comer, a renowned child psychiatrist, reinforces the imperative: "Equity in education begins with inclusive parent involvement. By creating a culture that values diverse perspectives, schools lay the foundation for student success that resonates across communities" (*Leave No Child Behind: Preparing Today's Youth for Tomorrow's World*, 2004).

Chapter 7 is a voyage into the heart of equity, guided by the insights of visionary researchers. It unravels the intricate challenges faced by families from diverse backgrounds, and charts a course for fostering inclusive parental involvement practices. Through the prism of research, quotes, and real-world examples, this chapter equips educational public school leaders with the knowledge and tools to bridge the equity gap, nurturing an educational landscape where all voices are heard, valued, and empowered to contribute to the holistic growth and success of every student.

In the mission to bridge the equity gap, the beacon of inclusive parental involvement shines a light that dispels the shadows of disparity. As we empower diverse families to become architects of their children's success, we dismantle barriers and build bridges of opportunity, acknowledging that true equity is born from the collaborative efforts of educators, families, and communities.
—Nury Castillo Crawford

Chapter 8: Cultivating Empathy and Gratitude: Acknowledging the Leaders of Parental Involvement

In the intricate dance of education where the partnership between schools and families shapes the destiny of students, a deep well of empathy and gratitude flows. As we delve into the heart of *Together We Thrive: Engage, Involve, Empower!*, Chapter 8 celebrates the unwavering dedication of educational public school leaders, and extends a hand of gratitude for the monumental challenge of fostering meaningful parental involvement.

The Heartbeat of Empathy

Empathy stands as a cornerstone of effective parental involvement efforts. Dr. Mary Gordon, a renowned advocate for social-emotional learning, affirms that, "empathy bridges the gap between educators and families, creating a space where mutual understanding fosters collaborative partnerships that empower students to thrive" (*Roots of Empathy: Changing the World Child by Child*, 2005).

Empathy for multilingual and multicultural families is of paramount importance as schools aim to increase parental involvement. Understanding and appreciating the unique backgrounds, experiences, and challenges these families bring to the educational environment is essential for creating an inclusive and welcoming atmosphere. Empathy helps educators and administrators recognize that language barriers, cultural differences, and varying levels of familiarity with the education system can sometimes hinder engagement. By demonstrating empathy, schools can adapt their communication strategies, provide language support, and offer resources that resonate with the specific needs of these families. This not only encourages greater parental involvement, but also builds trust, fosters a sense of belonging, and sends a powerful message that every family's perspective is valued in the pursuit of educational excellence. Ultimately, empathy serves as a foundation for effective collaboration, stronger partnerships, and improved outcomes for all students, regardless of their cultural or linguistic background.

Nurturing Empathy within Schools

Fostering empathy within schools requires a deliberate commitment to creating a culture of care. Dr. Dacher Keltner, a psychologist and expert in the science of empathy, emphasizes that, "educational leaders who model empathetic behavior and prioritize emotional well-being cultivate an environment where families feel understood, valued, and inspired to actively engage" (*Born to Be Good: The Science of a Meaningful Life*, 2009).

Nurturing empathy within a school's community, particularly for multicultural parents, requires intentional efforts to foster understanding, respect, and inclusivity. Here are some strategies schools can implement to nurture empathy:

1. **Cultural Competence Training:** Provide cultural competence training for all staff members, including teachers, administrators, and support staff. This training helps educators better understand and appreciate the diverse backgrounds and experiences of multicultural families.

2. **Diverse Representation:** Ensure that the school's staff and leadership reflect the diversity of

the student body. Diverse role models and decision-makers within the school can help create an inclusive atmosphere.

3. **Multilingual Communication:** Offer information and communication in multiple languages to accommodate non-English-speaking parents. Translate important documents, newsletters, and announcements to make them accessible.

4. **Cultural Awareness Programs:** Organize cultural awareness programs and events that celebrate the various cultures within the school community. Encourage parents to share their traditions, foods, and stories.

5. **Parental Ambassadors:** Recruit parental ambassadors from diverse backgrounds who can serve as bridges between the school and their respective communities. These ambassadors can help facilitate communication and understanding.

6. Cultural Sensitivity Curriculum: Integrate a cultural sensitivity curriculum into the school's educational program to teach students about different cultures, traditions, and histories.

7. Parental Workshops: Offer workshops and seminars for parents that focus on cultural awareness, effective communication, and understanding the American education system. Provide a platform for parents to share their insights and experiences.

8. Cultural Exchanges: Organize cultural exchange activities where families can learn about and from one another's backgrounds. These could include potlucks, cultural festivals, and heritage month celebrations.

9. Open Dialogue: Encourage open and respectful dialogue between parents and school staff. Create spaces for parents to express their concerns, share their perspectives, and ask questions.

10. Collaborative Projects: Engage parents in collaborative projects that promote a sense of unity and shared purpose. This could involve parent-teacher committees, volunteer opportunities, or community service initiatives.

11. Inclusive Policies: Review and adjust school policies and practices to ensure they are inclusive and respectful of different cultures and backgrounds. This includes considering diverse perspectives in decision-making processes.

12. Resources and Support: Provide resources and support services to help multicultural families navigate the challenges they may face, such as access to healthcare, legal assistance, and housing support.

13. Feedback Mechanisms: Establish feedback mechanisms to solicit input from parents and community members. Act on the feedback received to demonstrate that their voices are valued.

14. Parental Education: Offer opportunities for parents to learn about their children's education, including workshops on helping with homework, understanding curriculum, and supporting college readiness.

To nurture empathy within a school's building for multicultural parents and the community, deliberate efforts are essential. Cultural competence training for all staff members helps create a deeper understanding and appreciation of diverse backgrounds. Diverse representation within the school's staff and leadership, combined with multilingual communication, demonstrates a commitment to inclusivity. Cultural awareness programs and events, parental ambassadors, and cultural sensitivity curricula foster a sense of belonging and respect. Furthermore, open dialogue, collaborative projects, and feedback mechanisms allow for meaningful exchanges and shared experiences. Inclusive policies and support services address specific needs, while parental education workshops and resources enhance parents' understanding of the education system. By embracing these strategies, schools can create an environment where empathy thrives, nurturing stronger relationships and partnerships with multicultural families, and fostering an inclusive and supportive educational community.

The Power of Gratitude

In the pursuit of transformative parental involvement, gratitude emerges as a powerful force. Dr. Robert Emmons, a leading researcher on gratitude, asserts that, "expressing gratitude to parents for their partnership in education not only strengthens the parent-school bond but also nurtures a positive atmosphere that enhances student motivation and achievement"

(*Thanks!: How the New Science of Gratitude Can Make You Happier,* 2007).

Gratitude plays a vital role in increasing parental involvement in schools as it fosters a sense of appreciation and recognition for parents' contributions to their children's education. When schools express gratitude toward parents for their engagement, whether through volunteer work, attending meetings, or supporting their child's learning at home, it reinforces a positive and welcoming atmosphere. This, in turn, encourages parents to become more actively involved, as they feel valued and integral to their child's educational journey. Gratitude also cultivates a culture of reciprocity, where parents are more likely to invest their time and efforts when they perceive that their contributions are acknowledged and respected. Ultimately, gratitude helps build stronger partnerships between schools and families, creating a supportive ecosystem that benefits students and the entire school community.

Cultivating a Culture of Gratitude

Educational leaders who champion gratitude create a ripple effect that cascades throughout the school community. I continually emphasize the role of leaders in this endeavor: "By acknowledging and appreciating the efforts of families, schools create a culture of gratitude that amplifies the impact of parental involvement, nurturing a sense of belonging and ownership" (*Engaging Families in Schools: Community and Systemic Perspectives*, 2016).

To cultivate a culture of gratitude within a school, it is essential to consistently acknowledge and celebrate the contributions of parents and community members. This can begin by recognizing and thanking parents for their involvement, whether through handwritten notes, verbal expressions of gratitude during meetings, or special events dedicated to celebrating their efforts. Schools can also create a "Gratitude Wall" or an online platform where teachers, administrators, and students can share messages of appreciation. Encouraging students to express gratitude to their parents for their support in their academic journey can be especially impactful. Additionally, schools can organize annual or seasonal appreciation events, inviting parents and community members to participate in recognition ceremonies. By consistently expressing gratitude and making it an integral part of the school's culture, educators can foster a sense of belonging, increase parental involvement, and create a positive and supportive environment for all stakeholders.

The Leaders' Journey: A Reflection

As we reflect on the journey of educational public school leaders, it becomes evident that the challenges they navigate in fostering parental involvement are monumental. The dedication, perseverance, and unwavering commitment required to bridge gaps and nurture partnerships are profound. Dr. James P. Comer's words echo: "Leaders who embark on the path of parent involvement undertake a transformative journey that shapes not only the educational landscape but also the lives of countless students and families" (*Leave No Child Behind: Preparing Today's Youth for Tomorrow's World,* 2004).

A Unified Salute

In a collective symphony of gratitude and empathy, educators, parents, and communities unite to salute the tireless efforts of educational public school leaders. Dr. Karen Mapp encapsulates the sentiment: "To the leaders who champion parent involvement, your dedication propels a ripple of positive change that reverberates far beyond the classroom, nurturing an educational landscape where collaboration and partnership thrive" (*Beyond the Bake Sale: The Essential Guide to Family-School Partnerships,* 2007).

Chapter 8 is an ode to empathy and gratitude, a tribute to the leaders who rise to the challenge of nurturing meaningful parental involvement. Through a lens of empathy and a heart of gratitude, this chapter acknowledges the pivotal role of educational public school leaders in shaping partnerships that transcend boundaries, bridge gaps, and elevate the educational journey of every student. As we approach the final chapters, we delve into recommendations that further amplify the impact of parental involvement, transforming it into an enduring legacy of growth and success.

In the garden of education, cultivating empathy and gratitude nurtures the roots of parental involvement, where leaders bloom as stewards of growth and inspiration. Just as flowers reach for the sun, these leaders elevate the landscape of learning, reminding us that their tireless efforts are the petals that adorn the bouquet of student achievement.

—Nury Castillo Crawford

Chapter 9: Sustaining and Scaling Up: Strategies for Long-Term Impact in Parental Involvement

As our exploration

of *Together We Thrive:*

Engage, Involve,

Empower! reaches its zenith, the focus shifts to

sustaining and scaling the impact of parental

involvement. Chapter 9 delves into strategies that extend

the legacy of collaboration between schools, families, and

communities, ensuring that the transformative effects of

meaningful parental involvement endure and expand

over time.

Fostering a Culture of Continuity

Long-term impact necessitates a culture of continuity where parental involvement becomes an embedded part of the educational ethos. Dr. Anne T. Henderson advocates for this approach, "Creating a culture that treats parent involvement as an ongoing commitment, rather than a short-term project, ensures that the partnerships forged today remain vibrant and sustainable for generations to come" ("A New Wave of Evidence: The Impact of School, Family, and Community Connections on Student Achievement," 2002).

Dr. Anne Henderson's concept of fostering a culture of continuity emphasizes the importance of maintaining a cohesive and consistent approach to education throughout a child's academic journey, from early childhood through high school. This concept underscores the idea that educational success is not achieved in isolation, but is a cumulative effort that involves educators, parents, and communities working together across the years. It encourages schools and families to establish a seamless and collaborative partnership, ensuring that the strategies, expectations, and support systems in place remain consistent as students progress through different grade levels. By maintaining this continuity, students benefit from a stable and supportive environment that recognizes their unique needs and provides them with a coherent and well-rounded education. Dr. Henderson's philosophy highlights the profound impact of long-term, sustained collaboration between schools and families on students' academic achievements and overall well-being.

This concept of fostering a culture of continuity has significant implications for both schools and families. For schools, it means adopting a holistic and long-term approach to education, where the educational journey is viewed as a cohesive continuum rather than isolated stages. It encourages consistent communication, alignment of curriculum and expectations, and sustained engagement with families over the years. Schools need to create structures and policies that support this continuity, such as ensuring smooth transitions between grade levels and actively involving parents in decision-making processes.

For families, this approach promotes a sense of partnership with the school that extends beyond individual academic years. It encourages parents to stay engaged, share insights, and participate in their child's education throughout their school life. Families become more aware of the school's values, expectations, and resources, allowing them to provide more effective support at home.

Implementing this concept with fidelity involves establishing clear ongoing communication channels between schools and families, such as regular meetings, newsletters, and digital platforms. It also requires a commitment from both parties to maintain consistent involvement and shared goals. Schools should offer resources and guidance to help parents navigate the educational journey, and ensure that every child receives a seamless and high-quality education from preschool through graduation. By prioritizing this culture of continuity, schools and families can work together to maximize the potential for student success and holistic development.

Professional Development for Sustainability

Educational public school leaders play a pivotal role in sustaining parental involvement through ongoing professional development. I am a huge advocate for the importance of equipping educators: "Providing teachers and staff with training on effective parent engagement strategies cultivates a knowledgeable and empathetic workforce, capable of nurturing partnerships that stand the test of time" (*Parent Engagement for Student Success: A Guide for K-12 Educators*, 2014).

As leaders, we play a pivotal role in instilling a growth mindset of teaching and learning among educational staff, and this mindset is integral for fostering ongoing improvement and innovation in schools. Leaders must recognize that professional development is not a one-time event but an ongoing journey that should be aligned with daily reflection on what is learned. By encouraging educators to reflect regularly on their teaching practices and to be open to experimentation and adaptation, leaders create a culture of continuous improvement. Furthermore, leaders need to actively monitor progress and provide constructive feedback to ensure that the professional development aligns with the school's goals and that teachers are effectively integrating new strategies into their classrooms. Equally important is celebrating progress, as acknowledging and appreciating the effort and growth of staff members fosters motivation and a positive learning environment. Ultimately, education leaders who champion a growth mindset among their staff create a culture of learning, adaptability, and collective excellence that benefits both educators and students alike.

Building Community Capacity

Sustainability finds its roots in the community where collective efforts amplify the impact of parental involvement. Dr. James P. Comer's principles of community building offer guidance: "By partnering with local organizations, businesses, and community leaders, schools enhance their capacity to create a supportive ecosystem where parents are empowered as partners in education" (*Leave No Child Behind: Preparing Today's Youth for Tomorrow's World*, 2004).

Local schools can implement this strategy by forging strong community partnerships and involving community members in educational initiatives. Schools can host regular community meetings to discuss educational priorities, challenges, and goals, ensuring that the broader community has a voice in shaping the educational landscape. Collaborative projects, such as community gardens, after-school programs, or literacy initiatives, can engage parents and community members in shared activities that benefit both students and the neighborhood. Moreover, schools can tap into local resources and expertise by inviting community members to participate as guest speakers, mentors, or volunteers. By fostering a sense of shared responsibility and investment in the school's success, local schools can create a sustainable ecosystem where parental involvement not only thrives but also becomes an enduring and integral part of the community's fabric.

Data-Driven Insights for Growth

Strategies for sustained impact are fortified by data-driven insights. Dr. Karen Mapp highlights the role of data: "Regularly assessing the effectiveness of parent involvement initiatives through data collection and analysis enables schools to make informed decisions, adapting and refining strategies to meet the evolving needs of families" (*Beyond the Bake Sale: The Essential Guide to Family-School Partnerships*, 2007).

Setting SMART (Specific, Measurable, Achievable, Relevant, Time-bound) goals is a crucial strategy for schools aiming to enhance parental involvement. While numerous aspects are essential in education, goal setting provides a clear and structured path to stay focused on specific objectives. For instance, a SMART goal for a school could be to increase parental attendance at parent-teacher conferences by 20 percent within the next academic year. This goal is Specific (increasing attendance), Measurable (by 20 percent), Achievable (with the right strategies), Relevant (as it impacts parental involvement), and Time-bound (within the next academic year).

To monitor these goals effectively, schools can implement several strategies. Teachers can regularly assess and track individual student progress toward achieving the goals, noting changes in parental involvement. Grade-level or subject-area teams can meet to discuss their strategies, share successes, and identify areas that require adjustment. At the school-wide level, administrators can hold regular meetings to review progress, share best practices, and allocate resources as needed. Data collection through surveys, attendance records, and feedback mechanisms can provide valuable insights. Ultimately, by employing SMART goals and establishing a robust monitoring system, schools can stay on track and continually improve their efforts to enhance parental involvement, aligning their initiatives with broader educational objectives.

Amplifying Student Leadership

Sustainability is advanced through the empowerment of students as leaders in their educational journey. Advocating and amplifying student voices is an important variable we should not overlook: "Encouraging students to take an active role in shaping parent involvement initiatives not only instills a sense of ownership but also nurtures a legacy of collaboration that extends beyond their years in the institution" (*Engaging Families in Schools: Community and Systemic Perspectives*, 2016).

Elevating and advocating for student voices in our schools is a powerful strategy for building a stronger community and increasing parental involvement. When students are encouraged to share their thoughts, concerns, and ideas, it fosters a sense of ownership and empowerment within the school environment. Student input can inform decision-making processes and lead to policies and practices that better align with their needs and aspirations. Moreover, when parents witness their children actively engaged in school affairs and given a platform to express themselves, it naturally encourages their own involvement. It creates a shared understanding between parents and students about the importance of education, leading to a more cohesive school community. For example, involving students in parent-teacher conferences or school board meetings, where they can discuss their experiences and needs, not only strengthens the parent-student-teacher partnership but also ensures that the educational environment is more inclusive and responsive to everyone's perspectives. By advocating for student voices, schools can create a community that values collaboration, communication, and collective efforts towards enhancing the educational experience for all.

Inviting and encouraging students to share their insights and become more involved in decision-making at local schools and school districts is essential for creating a more inclusive and responsive educational system. Here are some ways to achieve this:

1. **Student Advisory Committees:** Establish student advisory committees or councils at the school and district levels, where students can discuss and provide input on various aspects of school life, curriculum, policies, and extracurricular activities.

2. **Student Surveys:** Administer regular surveys to gather feedback from students on their educational experiences, needs, and concerns. Analyze the data and use it to inform decision-making processes.

3. **Student Representatives:** Include student representatives in school-level and district-level meetings, including parent-teacher associations, school board meetings, and administrative meetings, to ensure that student voices are heard.

4. **Open Forums:** Organize open forums or town-hall-style meetings where students can express their opinions, ask questions, and engage in constructive dialogue with school administrators and board members.

5. **Student-Led Initiatives:** Support and fund student-led initiatives and projects that address issues important to the student body. This could include organizing events, clubs, or advocacy campaigns.

6. **Youth Empowerment Programs:** Implement youth empowerment programs that provide students with leadership skills and

opportunities to take an active role in decision-making processes.

7. Student Portfolios: Encourage students to maintain portfolios or journals where they document their learning experiences, challenges, and achievements. Reviewing these portfolios can provide valuable insights.

8. Online Platforms: Create online platforms or forums where students can submit ideas, proposals, or concerns anonymously if they prefer, to ensure that all students have a voice.

9. Student-Teacher Conferences: Include students in conferences with teachers and parents to discuss their academic progress, goals, and areas where they need support.

10. Civic Education: Integrate civic education into the curriculum, teaching students about their rights and responsibilities and the importance of civic engagement.

11. School Newspapers or Blogs: Support student-run newspapers, blogs, or other publications that allow students to express their views and share insights with the school community.

12. Mentorship Programs: Establish mentorship programs where older students can guide and mentor younger peers, fostering a sense of responsibility and leadership.

13. Student Panels: Organize student panels or presentations during professional development days for teachers and staff to hear directly from students about their experiences.

14. Recognition and Awards: Recognize and celebrate students who actively contribute to decision-making and community improvement through awards and acknowledgments.

The Enduring Ripple Effect

Sustained impact in parental involvement culminates in a ripple effect that transcends boundaries. Dr. Joyce Epstein encapsulates the legacy: "When schools, families, and communities collaborate tirelessly over time, the impact radiates outward, touching lives, transforming communities, and creating a legacy of partnership that endures for generations" (*School, Family, and Community Partnerships: Your Handbook for Action*, 2019).

Chapter 9 marks the culmination of our journey, focusing on strategies that ensure the lasting impact of meaningful parent involvement. By fostering a culture of continuity, equipping educators, building community capacity, utilizing data-driven insights, and empowering students, educational public school leaders lay the foundation for a legacy of collaboration that echoes through the corridors of time. As we conclude this exploration, the final chapter beckons, inviting us to reflect on the transformative journey and embrace the future with renewed dedication to nurturing student success through the enduring power of partnership.

In the blueprint of educational evolution, sustaining and scaling up parental involvement forms the cornerstone of lasting impact, where strategies are the architects of a legacy that spans generations. Like builders of bridges to the future, we construct pathways of empowerment, acknowledging that the strength of these foundations is a testament to the vision, dedication, and foresight of educational leaders.

—Nury Castillo Crawford

Chapter 10: Embracing the Future: A Call to Action for Transformative Parental Involvement

As we stand at the precipice of possibility, the culmination of our journey through *Together We Thrive: Engage, Involve, Empower!* heralds a new beginning. Chapter 10 calls for a resounding call to action, inviting educational public school leaders to embrace the future with unwavering determination and elevate parental involvement to unprecedented heights.

A Vision of Possibility

The future of education is illuminated by the radiant potential of transformative parental involvement. Imagine an educational landscape where parents stand as true partners, guiding the trajectory of student success through active collaboration with schools and communities.

The ultimate vision for parental engagement in Latino families within our public school system is one of robust collaboration, equity, and empowerment. In this vision, Latino parents are active and respected partners in their children's education, with a deep understanding of the school system and their rights within it. Schools provide accessible, multilingual information, and resources that cater to the diverse needs of Latino families, ensuring they are informed and confident advocates for their children. The vision features culturally responsive curricula that celebrate Latino heritage and values, making students feel seen and valued. School leaders actively seek input from Latino parents on decisions related to curriculum, policies, and resource allocation, fostering a sense of ownership and inclusion. This vision also includes vibrant community partnerships where schools and local organizations collaborate to provide wraparound services and support for students and families, addressing socio-economic disparities. Ultimately, parental engagement among Latino families contributes to improved academic outcomes, reduced achievement gaps, and a more inclusive, equitable, and culturally rich educational system for all.

Building Bridges Beyond Boundaries

The call to action beckons us to transcend boundaries, creating bridges that connect homes, schools, and communities. Dr. Karen Mapp propels us forward: "Let us break down the walls that separate us and build bridges of collaboration that unite us, transforming education into a collective endeavor that empowers every child to flourish" (*Beyond the Bake Sale: The Essential Guide to Family-School Partnerships,* 2007).

As educational leaders in our public schools, our commitment to breaking down barriers must be unwavering. By dismantling silos and fostering cooperation among educators, parents, students, and the broader community, we can create an educational landscape where every child's unique potential is nurtured and celebrated. Let us prioritize inclusivity, equitable access, and a deep understanding of diverse perspectives, ensuring that no child is left behind. Through these collaborative efforts, we have the power to reshape the future of education, where the success of each student becomes a shared triumph, and the walls that once divided us crumble beneath the strength of our united commitment to educational excellence.

Nurturing a Legacy of Partnership

Embracing the future requires a commitment to nurturing a legacy of partnership that stands as a testament to our dedication. In my parental empowerment book, *Plant the Seeds Well ... Expect Wonders*, I share the importance of parents being fully committed throughout the entirety of their child's educational journey. In this book, I also share tips on how to connect with the school even if it feels like the school is not welcoming (i.e., not answering emails, not having someone speak Spanish or language of preference, and not having a contact to rely on such as a family center within the school). *Plant the Seeds Well ... Expect Wonders* is also available in Spanish, reflecting my desire to ensure all of our families feel seen, heard, and respected, which includes providing them with resources and information in a timely manner.

Amplifying Voices, Enriching Lives

The future we envision is one where voices are amplified and lives are enriched through meaningful parental involvement. Dr. Joyce Epstein paints a vibrant picture: "In this future, parents and educators stand side by side, forging a path of collaboration that shapes the destiny of students, creating a symphony of achievement that resounds through time" (*School, Family, and Community Partnerships: Your Handbook for Action*, 2019).

During the many opportunities I have been honored to have, I have presented and shared the importance of navigating the complex journey of increasing parental involvement in schools across America. Relationships matter in our field because we work to serve, lead, and empower people from the young ages of 4 (Pre-K) to grade 12. The three-tier formula is simplified by organizing the process into:

Engage: Engagement implies a level of interaction, interest, and commitment that goes beyond mere attendance and reflects a genuine partnership in supporting the child's learning journey. In my experience, this step can ultimately be the most important variable in the equation of increasing parental involvement as a whole. I like to think of this step in its most simplistic view. Let's think about this in terms that aren't necessarily school-based. When you meet someone personally who you believe you have a connection with, you get to know them. You communicate about things and events that aren't necessarily always your choice. That's how relationships work—it's a two-process that's not just about what you want to discuss or reiterate. Engaging people means you meet them where they are and focus on what they need as well. This builds trust, increases communication, and ultimately a positive relationship.

Involve: Involving parents in the context of public schools means including them in decision-making processes, committees, and activities related to school governance, curriculum development, and policy implementation. It signifies a deeper level of participation and influence where parents have a voice in shaping the educational environment and policies that impact their children's education. This can also include parents attending classroom- and school-wide events. For many of our parents who have been disengaged and disenfranchised, this is a huge milestone.

Empower: Empowering parents in public schools involves equipping them with the knowledge, skills, and resources necessary to actively advocate for their child's education and to engage constructively with the school system. This includes providing parents with information on educational practices, resources, and their rights within the school system. Empowerment emphasizes giving parents the confidence and agency to make informed decisions and play an active role in their child's academic success and overall well-being within the educational setting.

Embracing the Call

The call to action resounds with a clarion message: The future of education is intrinsically intertwined with the depth of our commitment to parental involvement. Dr. James P. Comer's words ignite our purpose: "Let us heed the call, embrace the future, and stand as architects of change, transforming education through our collective efforts to empower parents and nurture student success" (*Leave No Child Behind: Preparing Today's Youth for Tomorrow's World*, 2004).

In this final chapter, the journey comes full circle, embarking on a new stage of possibility and promise. The future beckons, inviting educational public school leaders to heed the call to action, to champion parental involvement, and to forge ahead with unwavering dedication. As we close this chapter, we extend our heartfelt gratitude to the leaders who tirelessly work to bridge gaps, amplify voices, and cultivate a legacy of partnership that propels education into a future of boundless potential.

As we stand at the crossroads of tomorrow, embracing the future becomes a resounding call to action, beckoning us to weave the fabric of transformative parental involvement into the tapestry of education. Just as pioneers chart new horizons, we navigate uncharted territories of possibility, recognizing that our collective efforts today will be the compass guiding the next generation towards a brighter, empowered, and enriched tomorrow.

—Nury Castillo Crawford

Conclusion: Empowering Partnerships for Lasting Impact

As we draw the curtain on our exploration through the pages of *Together We Thrive: Engage, Involve, Empower!*, we stand on the threshold of possibility and transformation. The journey we've undertaken, guided by the wisdom of pioneering scholars and illuminated by the stories of schools and communities, unveils a tapestry of collaboration that transcends barriers and ignites the flame of student success.

In the heart of this book, we've delved into the multifaceted aspects of parental involvement, exploring its impact on student achievement, the factors shaping engagement, strategies for meaningful collaboration, and the imperative of equity. We've witnessed the power of empathy, gratitude, and sustained effort in nurturing partnerships that flourish over time. Each chapter has been a step forward—a mosaic piece in the portrait of a collaborative educational landscape.

Throughout this journey, one resounding truth emerges: The foundation of lasting student success rests upon the shoulders of engaged parents, visionary educators, and supportive communities. The symphony of achievement we aspire to compose can only be orchestrated through a harmonious collaboration that bridges the gap between home and school, embracing diversity, fostering inclusivity, and championing equity.

As we turn the final page, we issue a call to action—a call that echoes through the halls of every school, resonates within every community, and reverberates in the hearts of educational public-school leaders across the nation. Let us heed this call to:

Embrace Empathy: Walk in the shoes of parents, understanding their aspirations, challenges, and dreams. Create an environment where their voices are heard, valued, and integrated into the educational discourse.

Foster Gratitude: Recognize the tireless efforts of parents and community members who dedicate their time and energy to supporting student success. Express gratitude for their partnership, acknowledging their vital role in shaping the educational journey.

Commit to Equity: Embrace diversity as a strength and strive for equitable parental involvement practices that empower every family, regardless of background or circumstance, to actively engage in their child's education.

Cultivate Continuity: Infuse parent involvement into the fabric of your school's culture, ensuring that collaboration is not a one-time endeavor but an enduring commitment that transcends generations.

Harness Data: Utilize data-driven insights to continuously assess and refine parental involvement initiatives, ensuring that strategies evolve to meet the evolving needs of families and students.

Empower Student Leaders: Empower students to take an active role in shaping parental involvement initiatives, cultivating leadership skills and fostering a legacy of partnership.

Forge Community Connections: Extend your reach beyond the school walls, partnering with local organizations, businesses, and community leaders to create a web of support that nurtures student success.

Champion Change: Stand as champions of change, propelling the vision of transformative parental involvement forward with unwavering dedication and commitment.

The story of education is far from static; it is a narrative of evolution, adaptation, and growth. The future we envision is a future where every child thrives, where partnerships flourish, and where the collaborative efforts of schools, families, and communities create a symphony of achievement that resounds through time.

As we wrap-up our learning for now, let us take these insights, lessons, and calls to action with us on our continued journey. Let us embrace the role of educational public school leaders with renewed purpose and unwavering dedication. Together, as we nurture meaningful parent involvement, we carve a path of empowerment, inspiration, and lasting impact for generations to come. The stage is set, the audience is waiting—let us continue to empower partnerships and nurture student success through the enduring power of collaboration.

Appendix: Research and Endnotes

This appendix provides a comprehensive list of the research and endnotes referenced throughout *Together We Thrive: Engage, Involve, Empower!*. The wealth of knowledge and insights contained in these sources has greatly enriched our exploration into the multifaceted aspects of parental involvement in education.

"Parent Engagement for Student Success: A Guide for K-12 Educators", 2014

Chase, Jordan. (2016). "Sampson County Schools continues to meet growth", *The Sampson Independent*.

Comer, J.P. (2004). *Leave No Child Behind: Preparing Today's Youth for Tomorrow's World*. Yale University Press.

Crawford, N.C. (2020). *Engaging Families in Schools: Community and Systemic Perspectives. Routledge.*

Crawford, N.C. (2020). *Plant the Seeds Well, Expect Wonders*

Emmons, R.A. (2007). *Thanks!: How the New Science of Gratitude Can Make You Happier. Houghton Mifflin Harcourt.*

Epstein, J., Sanders, M., Steven, S., Simon, B., Salinas, K., Jamson, N., VanVoorhis, F., Martin, C., Thomas, B., Greenfield, M., Hutchins, D., Williams, K. *School, Family, and Community Partnerships: Your Handbook for Action*

Epstein, J.L. (2010). *School, Family, and Community Partnerships: Preparing Educators and Improving Schools. Westview Press.*

Gándara, P.C. (2014). *The Bilingual Advantage: Language, Literacy, and the US Labor Market. Teachers College Press.*

Geller J., and Diemer, M. (2021). *Parent Involvement as a Lever for School Reform.*

Gordon, M. (2005). *Roots of Empathy: Changing the World Child by Child. The Experiment, LLC.*

Henderson, A.T., Mapp, K.L. (2002). "A New Wave of Evidence: The Impact of School, Family, and Community Connections on Student Achievement." National Center for Family and Community Connections with Schools.

Henderson, A.T., Mapp, K.L., Johnson, V.R., Davies, D. (2007). *Beyond the Bake Sale: The Essential Guide to Family-School Partnerships*. The New Press.

Hope Academy of Public Service. (2019). "Area School Study Haps Model." Retrieved from https://www.hpsdistrict.org/o/academy-of-public-service/article/94082

International Commission on the Futures of Education. (2021). "Reimagining Our Futures Together: A New Social Contract for Education

Ishimaru, A.M. (2019). *Equity Walks: Exploring Equity and Justice in School and Society*. Harvard Education Press.

Jeynes, W.H. (2007). "The Relationship Between Parental Involvement and Urban Secondary School Student Academic Achievement: A Meta-Analysis." *Urban Education*, 42(1), 82-110.

Keltner, D. (2009). *Born to Be Good: The Science of a Meaningful Life*. W.W. Norton & Co.

Jeynes, W.H. (2015). "A Meta-Analysis: The Effects of Parental Involvement on Minority Children's Academic Achievement.*" Education and Urban Society, 35*(2).

Ladson-Billings, G. (1994). *The Dreamkeepers: Successful Teachers of African American Children*. Jossey-Bass.

Lawrence-Lightfoot, S. (2003). *The Essential Conversation: What Parents and Teachers Can Learn from Each Other*. Ballentine Books

Mapp, K.L. (2007). *Beyond the Bake Sale: The Essential Guide to Family-School Partnerships*. The New Press.

Mapp, K.L. (2019). *Partnering with Families for Student Success: The Power of Organizing Together*. Harvard Education Press.

National Center for Educational Statistics in May 2023 via their report titled "Racial/Ethnic Enrollment in Public Schools

Paris, D. & Alim, H.S. (2017). "Culturally Sustaining Pedagogies: Teaching and Learning for Justice in a Changing World." Teachers College Press.

What Is Bronfenbrenner's Ecological Systems Theory? (2019, May 3). Retrieved August 6, 2019, from https://www.psychologynoteshq. com/ bronfenbrenner-ecological-theory/.

We extend our heartfelt gratitude to these scholars and researchers whose work has provided the foundation for our journey into the realm of transformative parental involvement. Their insights have guided us toward a deeper understanding of the intricate

dynamics that shape educational partnerships, and we

carry their wisdom forward as we continue to empower

partnerships and nurture student success through

collaboration, dedication, and unwavering commitment.

About the Author

Nury Castillo Crawford is an accomplished and esteemed figure in the field of education, boasting a remarkable track record of over 25 years as a transformational leader in the public education sector. Her journey as an educational leader has been characterized by a dedication to collaboration with community stakeholders to optimize resources and information for the students and families for which she passionately advocates. Over the course of 2 decades, she has worn various hats, serving as a teacher, school administrator, and district-level leader.

Nury's journey began in Peru, where she was born, before she emigrated to the United States as a young girl. Her personal experience instilled in her a deep appreciation for the value of education as a pivotal factor in ensuring the success of the nation's youth.

Beyond her educational roles, Nury is a visionary entrepreneur who passionately supports literacy. As a bilingual Latina, she takes immense pride in being the owner of 1010 Publishing, a small press in Georgia that annually disseminates approximately five bilingual books. Her commitment to literacy further extends to THE little BOOK SPOT, a multilingual bookstore she recently established in Metro Atlanta, complemented by a brick-and-mortar free library. Both of these entities were conceived with a singular goal: to enhance access to literacy and literacy-related resources, with a strong emphasis on bilingual and biliterate books that celebrate biculturalism and a sense of pride in one's ancestry and culture.

Nury's outstanding contributions to education and leadership have garnered national recognition. In 2022, she was honored as a national Latino leader and received the prestigious TUMI Award, celebrating the leadership of Peruvian Americans in the United States. This accolade joins a growing list of distinctions, including being named one of the "50 Most Influential Latinos" for 3 consecutive years, in 2019, 2020, and 2021. In addition, she was recognized as the National Educator of the Year by Mundo Hispanico.

Her impact extends beyond the realm of education. Nury was featured prominently in a national organization dedicated to elevating and empowering the Latino community in the United States, where she was celebrated as "The Hispanic Rising Star: The New Face of Power." She is a sought-after national speaker, addressing audiences on a variety of critical topics, such as parental involvement, education, mentoring, equity, and bilingualism. Her numerous authored books further cement her status as an influential voice in these areas, and she continues to share her expertise throughout the country, emphasizing the significant role Latinos play in American culture.

Nury's influence and expertise have not gone unnoticed by the media. She has been featured in national outlets, both in English and Spanish, including but not limited to ABC, NBC, CBC, NPR, T*he Atlanta Journal-Constitution* newspaper, *Mundo Hispanico* newspaper, numerous national blogs and podcasts as well as local television stations.

Beyond her professional accolades, Nury remains actively engaged with her audience through social media. She hosts a vibrant Facebook group, Latino Parents & Youth, and organizes monthly events with parents, both in person and virtually, drawing the engagement of thousands of parents annually. Her commitment to providing resources and information to parents has earned her national recognition for her success in empowering communities. Nury Castillo Crawford is not just an author; she is a multifaceted leader, educator, and advocate dedicated to making a profound impact on

the lives of the people she serves.

www.ingramcontent.com/pod-product-compliance
Lightning Source LLC
Chambersburg PA
CBHW050650270326
41927CB00012B/2966